The Art of
Performance

The Art of Performance

Towards a Theology of
Holy Scripture

FRANCES YOUNG

Darton, Longman and Todd
London

First published in 1990 by
Darton, Longman and Todd Ltd
89 Lillie Road, London SW6 1UD

British Library Cataloguing in Publication Data

Young, Frances M. (Frances Margaret), *1939–*
The art of performance.
1. Bible – Critical studies
I. Title
220.6

ISBN 0–232–51779–7

Manuscript on cover is taken from *Motetti Novi e Chanzoni Franciose a Quatro Sopra Doi*, edited by Andrea Antico, and used by permission of Editions Minkoff.

Phototypeset by
Input Typesetting Ltd, London SW19 8DR
Printed and bound in Great Britain by
Courier International Ltd, Tiptree, Essex

To JGD
with respect
and gratitude

Contents

Acknowledgements

I am grateful for the encouragement and assistance of my colleagues David Ford and John Eaton, both of whom read drafts as the chapters were produced. The A. S. Peake memorial lecture at the Methodist Conference 1989, and in the same year the Reid lectures at Westminster College, Cambridge made use of material in this volume, and I am grateful for subsequent discussions which alerted me to a number of significant matters. The substance of the first chapter was originally drafted in 1986 as a paper for a Graduates Reunion Conference in Birmingham, which was also a tribute and farewell to the retiring Edward Cadbury Professor, J. Gordon Davies. His successor would like to dedicate this volume to him in gratitude for years of encouragement, and a regime which allowed freedom to develop as scholar, teacher and minister.

FRANCES YOUNG

Prologue

How can we treat the Bible as Holy Scripture if it is to be
subjected to literary or historical criticism like any other book?

How can we submit to the Bible's judgment on us if we
insist on submitting it to our critical judgment?

How can we respect and appropriate beliefs and injunctions
which we know were the result of past cultural conditioning?

How can we regard the Bible as having sacred authority if
it is found to be story and fable not history?

How can we live in and worship with the Bible – how can
we 'perform' the Bible—in a modern world so different from
the past which produced and used it?

To state such questions is to highlight the contradiction
between the customary ritual honouring of the scriptures in
liturgy and the methods of studying the Bible and comment-
ing upon it generally accepted in circles which care about a
certain academic respectability. It is also to indicate the current debate within academia. Those in the know will recognise
that the questions point to the crisis within modern theology
represented by so many books on the theory of interpretation
(or 'hermeneutics'), by the emergence of 'narrative-theology'
and the demands for so-called *praxis* in liberation-theology,
indeed by the developing reaction against 'historico-critical
method' within the domain of biblical scholarship itself, a
reaction at least partially fuelled by new approaches to literary criticism.

This book arises from a hunch that many of the problems
now at the forefront in Biblical Studies and Hermeneutics
might be illuminated by attending to the use and understanding of the Bible found in the early Church Fathers, those who

1

in the early centuries determined which books belonged to scripture and how they were to be read. But that fundamental argument is complemented by the use of the analogy with performance of drama and music. For such performance is a kind of ritual, with many of the same problems of appropriation and interpretation built into the situation.

Writing this book has been a re-vitalising experience, a feeling of being carried into unexpected places by the inspiration of some god – what the Greeks would have called *enthousiasmos* or divine in-breathing. This strangely creative sense arises from the impulse received from the generative power of that musical analogy or metaphor.

Some years ago I exploited Arthur Koestler's book *The Act of Creation*[1] in *Can these Dry Bones Live?*[2] There he describes what he calls "bisociative thinking" as the basis of all creative activities, artistic originality, scientific study, even the good joke. He analyses the "spontaneous flash of insight which shows a familiar situation or event in a new light":

> Pythagoras, according to tradition, is supposed to have discovered that musical pitch depends on the ratio between the length of vibrating chords – the starting-point of mathematical physics – by passing in front of the local blacksmith on his native island of Samos, and noticing that rods of iron of different lengths gave different sounds under the blacksmith's hammer. Instead of ascribing it to chance, one suspects that it was obscure intuition which made Pythagoras stop at the blacksmith's shop.

Koestler discerned that that kind of intuition works by "the unlikely marriage of cabbages and kings – of previously unrelated frames of reference or universes of discourse – whose union will solve the previously insoluble problem". I suggested then that hermeneutics requires a similar flash of insight which enables the bringing together of the world of the text and our own lives. But here and now Koestler's

1. Hutchinson, 1964; Pan Books, 1970.
2. SCM, 1982.

2

insight illuminates the process whereby an unexpected analogy has enabled creative leaps.

So as the writing got under way, the analogy with performance – particularly musical performance, though opera or drama sometimes takes over – took off and began to stimulate new insights in a remarkable way. If it begins to seem like 'compositional allegory' by the end, that will itself provide an example of the potential of seeing one thing under the image of another.

I should insist that the analogy is meant to be no more than that; for the potential for misunderstanding undoubtedly exists. This is not intended to be a study of music in the patristic period[1] and positive use of the musical metaphor in the Fathers is more significant for my purposes than their moralistic polemic against it; nor is it meant to be a philosophy of music or a theological evaluation of it.[2] I am well aware of the fact that the interpretation of music is highly controversial – if it comes to that, so is the interpretation of the Bible – but even if it is not proper to speak of it as a 'language' or as having 'content', it seems nevertheless to be some form of communication, and performance is of its essence. If the objection is raised that I have overlooked the fact that music may sometimes be demonic, my analogy still holds – so can ideological performance of the Bible!

So the book explores what is involved in performance so as to illuminate the process of appropriating the Bible in the modern world, though its substantive content is an exploration of patristic use of the Bible, with the questions and dilemmas of modern Biblical Studies in mind. The first chapter grapples with the most obvious and topical analogy: does historical reconstruction matter for 'authentic' performance of classical works from the past? This enables some introduction to the present methodological crisis. Thereafter ideas arising from patristic approaches are intertwined with the performance theme.

1. See J. McKinnon, *Music in Early Christian Literature*, CUP, 1987.
2. I am grateful for the recent study by Ivor H. Jones, *Music: A Joy for Ever*, Epworth, 1989.

1

Interpretation and the Quest for Authenticity

A. S. Peake was a 'performer'. He 'performed' scripture, in his lectures, his writings and the pulpits of Primitive Methodist Churches. His one-volume commentary became the companion which enabled hundreds of others to become 'performers' week by week in the life, worship and teaching of untold numbers of Church communities. This 'star' performer had a 'patron', Mr W. P. Hartley, who financed his 'performance' and enabled him to pass on his techniques to pupils, those in ministerial training at what became Hartley College. Gradually his ideal of 'authentic performance' won ground, despite opposition, fear and uncertainty. The 'original' meaning of a biblical text was the 'true' meaning. The biblical revelation lay in the events and experiences to which the texts gave witness. This revelation was 'progressively' revealed, and the history of movement from primitive ideas to monotheism could be traced from close critical attention to the texts and the process of their formation. This was the key to the meaning of scripture, and so to the possibility of witness in every generation, witness to what God had done in history. Historico-critical method enabled the 'performance' of scripture.

> Throughout that long and heroic life, he remained true to his great task of bringing down the close study of the Word of God from heaven to men. . . Like a true musician, he made others share what his own ear could detect, the most delicate harmonies and the broad sweeping effects; while,

4

as those who knew him best were aware, he could frame out of three sounds not a fourth, but a star.[1]

For a century and more, the Bible has been problematic and yet remained fundamental to Christian theology. For a while the brilliant exposition of masters like A. S. Peake obscured the nature of the challenge of biblical criticism to traditional use of the Bible, though the fundamentalist response was always there if often dismissed or disregarded. Increasingly reaction is setting in, and new methods present a challenge to long-standing scholarly assumptions. How can the 'rationalism' of the critical tradition respond to the needs of theology? Is there not an inevitable tension between the Bible as the Word of God and the Bible as an object of historical research?

The novels of the Jewish writer, Chaim Potok, have a disturbing ability to hold up a mirror to problems at the heart of Christian theology, and allow us to see the outline sharpened up and exaggerated. When a Jew belonging to a close community in New York discovers biblical criticism, and in his excitement decides to go and study Torah with the Goyim, the cruciality of the challenge is dramatically enhanced by the coincidence that just then news of the Holocaust begins to filter out: German Goyim are responsible for both, so how can they not both be destructive of religion? Yet the novel, *In the Beginning*,[2] is not content with such a simplistic answer. The challenge of modernism has to be faced if truth is to be served. Continued faithfulness depends on risk and vulnerability. Even without the personal cost of offending family and community just at that critical time, the kind of fundamentalist reaction so painful and familiar within Christianity would have created the greater anguish, simply because the Pentateuch lies nearer the heart of Judaism.

Out of the lesser but none the less personally painful experiences of many exposed to biblical criticism, has been born a widespread uneasiness, a sense that we have to move on into a

1. W. F. Lofthouse, quoted in John T. Wilkinson, *Arthur Samuel Peake*, Epworth, 1971, p. 195.

2. Heinemann, and Penguin, 1976.

postcritical stage. The burgeoning of interest in structuralism, hermeneutical method and canon criticism can be seen as the direct result not only of the impact of other disciplines on biblical study, but also of the anxiety inherent in the subject itself that in the end it has not produced religiously significant results, and has undermined the Bible's place as Holy Scripture. The basic argument of this book is that despite these reactions, the validity of biblical criticism remains, alongside and together with the doctrine that the Bible is the Word of God.

Since the early 1970s within the field of biblical studies, dissatisfaction has been expressed. The biblical theology movement began to run into the sands even as the present writer began the study of theology in the 1960s, and New Testament study, particularly study of its theology, began to seem fragmented and increasingly complex. There is no doubt people were beginning to feel that traditional methods had been worked to death, and American PhD factories were looking for new topics. It was into a kind of vacuum – or at least feeling of uncertainty – that structuralist exegesis burst on to the scene. It took most of us a little while to wake up to what was happening, and even now traditional biblical studies continue to be taught, and the new approaches have scarcely affected syllabuses in many places. There is a fairly widespread feeling of suspicion about structuralism in English circles devoted to traditional scholarship – you may have noticed press coverage of the split in the Cambridge English Faculty in the 1970s on precisely this issue. Besides, most specific structuralist essays are incredibly complex, and the whole thing has become ever more esoteric and seemingly more liable to being abstruse and irrelevant than more traditional approaches. Perhaps not surprisingly, structuralism is already giving way to poststructuralist movements in literary circles, so that already biblical studies are in danger of having to run to catch up the ever-moving train of intellectual fashion. Yet in some ways these developments are very exciting, and structuralism at least allows one to see many things in a new light.

Structuralism developed out of linguistic theory, and has

been applied by analogy to myth, narrative and literary texts, thus affecting anthropological and historical studies as well as literary criticism and many other fields within the humanities. Several useful and sympathetic accounts have been given of its procedures: particularly to be recommended is John Barton, *Reading the Old Testament*;[1] and Robert Morgan (with John Barton), *Biblical Interpretation*,[2] shows how it relates to the story of modern biblical studies. It is not proposed to offer a rival account here, since these books already provide clear exposition of a very complex matter, but enough must be said to give some indication of what the movement is all about.

The basic idea is that meaning is a function of contrast within a given system. Words and sentences do not have any 'inherent' meaning – the meaning is a function of the system or structure of which they form a part. So to use an example from the anthropologist Mary Douglas,[3] dirt is "matter out of place". It implies "a set of ordered relations and contravention of that order". Dirt is never a unique isolated event. Where there is dirt there is system. Dirt is a by-product of a systematic ordering and classification of matter, in so far as ordering involves rejecting inappropriate elements. Dirt is a relative idea. So "culture, in the sense of the public, standardised views of a community, mediates the experience of individuals. It provides in advance some basic categories, a positive pattern in which ideas and values are tidily ordered . . . Cultural categories are public matters." And the medium by which culture is 'carried' is language: learning to name things is learning to classify them.

So structuralists argue that all structures by which meaning is generated can be analysed in terms of opposites – they have a *binary* character. So 'weeds' are weeds because they are the opposite of 'flowers', and while they may be as pretty as any other flower, they are not acceptable because they are flowers out of place. One learns competence in one's own language – like learning the rules of a game of chess. The variety of original statements that can be made within the system is

1. DLT, 1984.
2. OUP, 1988.
3. *Purity and Danger*, Routledge and Kegan Paul, London, 1966.

enormous, but the rules of the system can still be discerned and analysed. Similarly, in the realm of story-telling it is possible to discern the system, and how the story functions by exploiting the rules.

In other words, applied to literature, structuralism shows *how* texts work. It all began with an analysis of folk-tales by Vladimir Propp which appeared in Russian in 1928. Hundreds of folk-tales were shown to be reducible to a limited set of 'stock' characters who had standard 'roles' to play in the story. The roles depend on their 'opposition' to one another. This consistency meant it was possible to express the tales in algebraic formulae. A story which contravened the rules one somehow recognised to be not a proper folk-tale. From this beginning, analysis of literary texts began to flourish, particularly in French circles.

Structuralism, then, is really a theory about literature, but it has been exploited as a method of exegesis. It is supposed to uncover the 'meaning' of the story through its analysis. Many papers, it must be admitted, leave one with the feeling, 'Well, so what?' Or, 'Oh really, I'd never have guessed it!' In other words, if it is analysis proper it cannot get you anywhere, and if it is exploited to produce 'meaning' it can be a convenient tool for covering up imaginative guesses in quasi-scientific formulae. It often seems to be a technique which allows people to play with texts without regard to any of the usual technical skills required – you have no need of the original Hebrew or Greek, you need not know the background, or the sources, or the redaction, or the culture, or the intention of the original author. The meaning is in the 'universal' narrative structures, and the proper study is the text as it exists now. You can only discover what the story is really about by looking for these meanings which are not explicitly stated but implicit in the structures. Charts and diagrams are a better medium for conveying what it is all about than exegesis.

Two things about structuralist exegesis have offended the traditional biblical exegete. The first is the overt hostility to other methods, and the campaigning tone of it all. Nothing else will do. Everyone else has been misguided. Structuralism can be a kind of intellectual imperialism. Those who have espoused it have turned on the critical hand which in a sense has fed them. Secondly, structuralists often appear entirely arbitrary in the way they approach the text as it stands now. They choose a passage, and determine its length to suit the patterns they have succeeded in discerning. They seem sometimes to impose patterns rather than discern them, and to be indulging in a game not unlike the allegorists of the patristic and medieval period. You can (almost) make the text mean anything you like, as long as you can produce a pretty diagram or algebraic formula. To some extent this reaction has been deliberately provoked – it is the shock tactics of the controversialist that many structuralists have liked to adopt. Can we give a more balanced assessment?

The structuralist attack has been upon the critical principle that has so long operated, namely that the meaning is what the original meant, and the original expressed the intention of the author. It has been assumed that if you can prove that Isaiah did not intend a Messianic prediction in 7:14 (the Immanuel passage), then that cannot have been the meaning but must have been read in later. Hypotheses about what Isaiah was referring to are then advanced in order to discern the original meaning of the text – what Isaiah intended. There is a sense in which the whole of what we call the 'historico-critical' approach has depended upon ascertaining authorial intention, and on the assumption that that provides the meaning. What has obscured that is the discovery that often we cannot be sure who the author was, that the texts are better regarded as community productions, and so on. But suppose the structuralists are right that the meaning of texts inhere in their structures and not in the authorial intention, traceable or not. Increasingly it seems that we need a 'multi-layered' view of what meaning is, and that the insights of both sides must be valued.

As I have previously suggested elsewhere,[1] debates about meaning in everyday life can throw light on our problem. No-one can make statements mean anything they like, because

---

1. *Meaning and Truth in 2 Corinthians*, SPCK, 1987, pp. 85ff.

language is in the public domain, as structuralists have insisted. Meaning 'inheres' in language – at least through shared cultural conventions and common rules of the game. So the following reactions to a statement are conceivable:

1. 'You said so-and-so.' 'No, I did not. I said so-and-so.'

The original statement has been re-phrased, and the originator of the statement objects to the re-phrasing because it does not convey what was intended. The hearer has to admit to having misunderstood. So despite the challenge of structuralism, we do normally grant the originator of the statement the right to adjudicate about its meaning.

2. 'You said so and so.' 'Oh, did I? That's not what I meant. What I meant to say was so-and-so.'

The original statement has been repeated. The originator of the statement agrees that the repetition is accurate, but suddenly recognises that it was inadequate as a statement of what was intended. Another attempt to convey the meaning is made. So we normally recognise that linguistic use and meaning are not necessarily identical, though clearly we always try to get as close as possible to articulating what is really meant. We normally admit also that there are variant ways of expressing meaning, that not all are as adequate as each other, and once more that the author of the statement has the right to adjudicate between more or less adequate attempts to express the meaning intended. However, we have to be cautious when applying this to texts, for it is the source of what has been called the 'intentional fallacy', namely that it is possible for a literary critic to know better than the author of a text what the author intended to say as distinct from what he succeeded in saying.

3. 'You said so-and-so.' 'Oh, yes. I did not have that in mind when I spoke. But of course what I said could mean that.'

Here the hearer has had insight into potential meaning of which the originator of the statement had been entirely unconscious. In a case like this, further discussion about whether the proposed meaning is possible or not does not depend upon the intention of the author, but on the potential of the linguistic statement made. The author could conceivably express reservations about the proposed meaning, and give reasons why it does not seem possible to interpret it that way. But so could anyone else. In the end the originator of the statement does not have the last word. In fact, if he is T. S. Eliot, he may refuse to participate in the discussion, and say that everyone has the right to understand it their own way. The adjudicator is likely to be a third party, and the outcome of the adjudication would depend upon the fact that language is in the public domain, and it is not private or esoteric. It is a matter of discussion whether the statement could objectively carry one meaning or the other, and the argument can only be settled if good reasons are advanced for one view or another. If language were private or esoteric no communication would be possible, and no debate about meaning could occur.

4. 'You said so-and-so.' 'Well, not exactly. You see when I use such-and-such a word, it has such-and-such associations for me. So the statement has a lot more overtones than you suggest.'

Despite the fact that language belongs to public culture, an individual or group may use language in an idiosyncratic way, so constituting a sub-culture. Then there are factors involved which only the author of the statement has access to. The audience is at a disadvantage until informed of these factors, and communication will only be half successful until this extra information is conveyed. On the other hand, an author might deliberately not use the ways of expression that come most naturally, but deliberately 'translate' into the 'hearer's' language. The conversation would then go:

'You said so-and so.' 'Yes. But I would not choose to put it that way. I was trying to express it in a way that you would find easier to grasp.'

The ensuing discussion would then clearly involve dialogue about one another's language. All cross-cultural communication will involve something along these lines, even if a common language is being used. The same phrases may mean

11

utterly different things to different people depending upon the total context in which they are used, the way they have been used in past communication with another group, and so on.

Now clearly debates about the meaning of a text cannot follow the same course. As many[1] have pointed out, following the hermeneutical approach of Paul Ricoeur, the text takes on a life of its own when it leaves the author, and the author is no longer present to discuss what was meant: "the writing-reading relation is not a particular case of the speaking-hearing relation". Dialogue is not possible. On the other hand, the complex nature of language communication remains unchanged. The author did consciously mean something, we presume, and the original intention of the author bears upon the question of meaning, no matter how difficult it may be to discern what it was. Some meanings the author would rule out of court, and sometimes it is possible to provide good reasons for being sure that that would be the case by careful attention to the whole of an author's output, or context, or whatever. You can sometimes demonstrate beyond contradiction that the author did not mean so-and-so. If that is the case, can there be any justification for proposing that the meaning of the text is what the author clearly did not intend? You cannot make a text mean anything you like, and the author's intention does bear upon the question of meaning, even if it does not exhaust it.

Now if this is the case, whatever the difficulties involved, and we are more and more aware of the difficulties and less and less confident we can be sufficiently objective to be sure we are right – nevertheless, the aim of biblical criticism to ascertain the original form of the text and the original intention of the author is not to be despised. It is an essential component in the discussion of meaning, and cannot be cavalierly dismissed as structuralists have tried to assert.

Furthermore, if we take up again the issue concerning the cultural aspects of language – an essential ingredient in structural linguistics, in fact – it should be immediately clear that

1. e.g. J. G. Davies, 'Subjectivity and Objectivity in Biblical Exegesis', *Bulletin of the John Rylands Library*, 66 (1983), pp. 44–53.

the 'philological' method cannot be dismissed. Words and sentences, gestures and intonation, mean what they mean within a cultural system. The texts with which we have to deal come from a cultural system different from our own. It is not simply a question of learning Greek or Hebrew in a somewhat mechanical way – it is trying to get into a cultural-linguistic whole which the author and his original addressees shared and which we do not.

So the seemingly endless hypotheses about influence and counter-influence – questions like 'how Gnostic is John's Gospel?' – are to do with grasping the total cultural complex of the texts. Which cultural 'sub-group' does this language come from? It will make a great deal of difference to the way we understand its meaning – even if we are not tied to 'author-ial intention'. Language is in the public domain. But how public is the language of the New Testament writings in terms of the historical period and society in which they emerged? If it is not 'public', in what way is it esoteric, the language of a sub-group? Is it a kind of translationese? Is it a dialect like 'Indian English'? What does the language refer to? What are the overtones of the vocabulary? How would people respond to the imagery? What kind of social customs are implied by the verbal niceties or descriptions of behaviour? To interpret the meaning of texts from the past involves 'cross-cultural communication', whether we like it or not. And while again we must be less and less confident we can find all the answers, the process which we refer to when we speak of 'biblical criticism' is quite simply unavoidable. Recent developments in 'sociological study' of the New Testament are a necessary corollary of trying to understand the meaning of the texts, and the insights of structuralist anthropology have made a considerable contribution to our ability to understand features of biblical culture, like sacrifice and purity rituals, in a much deeper way.

Another feature of structural linguistics proves again the necessity of a historical approach to the question of meaning. The initial distinction made in linguistics was between 'dia-chronic' and 'synchronic' study: etymology, the origins and developmental history of words was to be rejected in favour of studying current usage. So it became clear that biblical theology had been too 'etymological' in a false way. It was James Barr's book, *The Semantics of Biblical Language*,[1] which alerted the scholarly world to this kind of problem. But if the important thing is 'synchronic' study, then Greek usage then, and even the usage of the underlying Aramaic then, at the time when the texts were written, is a vital component in understanding what might be legitimate interpretations. There are features of structuralism which should *encourage* not discourage the traditional enterprise.

Another feature of structuralism which falls into this category is its stress on the necessity of proper identification of genre. To put it in terms familiar in our own literary culture: a novel is different from a biography which is quite different from a folk-tale. In the latter case the structures are likely to be different, but in the former, although structures may be remarkably similar, a correct reading of the text depends upon recognising the distinction: this is well illustrated by the case of the correspondents who used to write to Mrs Dale[2] as a real person. Competence in reading literature depends upon accurate genre recognition.

Now the question all historical criticism has been concerned with is exactly this: how are we to be competent to read texts from another culture? How are we to identify the genres that were acceptable and recognisable and readable then? Can we spell out the features of such genres? The issue of the date and meaning of the Book of Daniel is closely bound up with the question of what genre to assign it to. The discovery of the genre 'apocalyptic' and the careful spelling out of its characteristic features has been fundamental to the critical reading of many passages in the New Testament and the discovery that treating the texts as literal predictions is to misunderstand them. This can only be done by careful historical research. A parallel question concerns Jonah: is this work to be read as history or fiction or what? The point I wish to make is that the principles of the structuralist very often

1. OUP, 1961.
2. *Mrs Dale's Diary* was a long-running radio series on BBC.

support the very thing that they are attacking, and that even if structuralism were to become more central to biblical study than it has succeeded in being so far, this could not be the end of traditional historical criticism. The interests and concerns of biblical criticism will remain fundamental to any responsible biblical study. We need to seek a marriage with new literary methods rather than continued hostilities, and increasingly this is being recognised.

But to pursue the question of genre naturally leads into another postcritical movement which has caused a good deal of discussion among biblical scholars, and has directly arisen out of dissatisfaction with the kind of criticism which had begun to seem both a dead-end and hostile to Holy Scripture: I refer to canon criticism. It seemed that the effect of biblical criticism had been to cause fragmentation. The drive to get back to the original led to the disintegration of texts into sources, because as wholes the texts did not seem to cohere. The detective work which tried so hard to reconstruct the historical details, background, precise situation, the particularities to which the texts refer, had led to the exploitation of contradictions and incoherences, the discernment of fundamental diversity.

So it was now recognised that the unity of the biblical witness could not be established by historical criticism, and that biblical theology had been too confident of a whole lot of untenable presuppositions. True, redaction-criticism began to try and discern the kind of intention the compilers had in making their compilations – so the theology of Luke became a matter of much discussion, rather than the reconstruction of proto-Luke. But redaction-criticism also reinforced the special characteristics of different 'theologies' within the biblical canon. In the face of this focus on diversity came the insistence that the 'canon' of scripture must provide the context in which meaning is sought. B. S. Childs[1] insisted that the final canonical form of the text is what should be the centre of attention for interpretation, and the literature should be read

1. *Introduction to the Old Testament as Scripture*, SCM, 1979.

as 'canon'. To put it into structuralist terms – the proper genre is the canon.

Like structuralism, canon criticism has been highly critical of the historical criticism which preceded it. And it has provoked some very violent reactions among biblical scholars – notably James Barr.[1] One of the most urgent questions if this type of interpretation is to take place is – which canon? There is a Hebrew canon, eventually produced within the Jewish community. There is an ecclesiastical canon comprising many more books in their Greek form, and with the addition of what we call the New Testament. There is the Protestant canon, which anachronistically accepted the Jews' Hebrew canon for the Old Testament, and treated the rest as deutero-canonical or apocryphal. One of the great strengths of the historico-critical movement has been the ability to transcend these different canons – Jews and Christians, Catholics and Protestants, have been able to engage in a common enterprise, and so in principle has the agnostic, because there is a shared methodology, a shared set of presuppositions about what texts mean – namely that their meaning lies in the original form of the text and in the intention of the original writer. Once you urge canonical interpretation, loyalty to different canonical traditions will inevitably cause divisiveness. Is Psalm 8 to be interpreted according to the Christological version of Hebrews 2? Are we to permit a Messianic reading of the Old Testament such as the early church indulged in?

Not only is there a problem about which canon, but there are problems about the interpretation of the canon as a whole. Lutheran scholarship has for a long time discussed the 'canon-within-the-canon', recognising that some parts of it appear to fall short of the high doctrine of other parts: Luther's statement that James is "a right strawy epistle – Christ is not taught therein" is well-known. Is 'justification by faith', or 'Christ', or what, the 'key' to the canon? Those who formed the canon did not approach it in those terms. The historical process of canon formation is something of which we need to be particularly conscious if we are to make these claims, and

1. *Holy Scripture: Canon, Authority, Criticism*, OUP, 1983.

16

the principle of apostolic authorship or whatever, is not going to seem very satisfactory as a way of understanding the canon as a whole, given the grave historical difficulties in accepting it. It may be that the principle of apostolic authorship was never the firm criterion scholars have supposed, but even so the question remains, and it is a serious one for Protestants: Are we tied to the view of the canon which those who formed it had? In the next chapter the historical formation of the canon will be examined as part of a discussion of what kind of a thing the canon is.

The rise of canon criticism is closely connected with the demise of biblical theology, a point discussed by Barr and Barton.[1] It has the virtue of taking seriously the canonical context of the writings with which we have to deal, and of being a serious attempt to reclaim the unity of the Bible. It purports to be theological, and yet in many ways it is a kind of literary theory not unlike the claims of structuralism – the issue is about identifying the correct genre, and therefore having the literary competence to read the texts.

In his book on the New Testament as canon, Childs has taken seriously many of the reactions to his original productions in the 1970s. Perhaps most important is his willingness to recognise the contribution that historical criticism must make if canon criticism is to function effectively. It is precisely because critical methods can identify earlier forms of the text, that the changing meanings as the works are integrated into the canon can be discerned. In the end, canon criticism is a kind of super-redaction criticism, taking the Bible as a whole rather than the individual writings in it. To that extent it inevitably owes much to all that has gone before. To work effectively, even in Childs' revised form, it depends on the more traditional analytical methods of biblical criticism, and it naturally leads to interest in the developing history of exegesis, the recognition of evolving or 'multiple' readings of texts. There is no one canonical reading.

In fact it is increasingly clear that we have to take seriously the development of exegetical traditions in the evolution not

1. *loc.cit.sup.*

only of postbiblical communities, both Jewish and Christian, but within the Bible itself. The New Testament self-consciously re-reads the Jewish scriptures in the light of their fulfilment in Christ, as much 'historical criticism' has revealed – a long bibliography concerned with the use of scripture in Gospels and Epistles could be assembled. But the same is true of what we call the Old Testament: Chronicles is a 'midrashic' rewriting of the Books of Samuel and Kings, prophetic books are compilations of material remembered and reinterpreted, Torah is the deposit of a long tradition of legal applications and development, and in quite precise ways the addition of interpretative comments to texts can be isolated in the scriptures.[1] This perception is the result of on-going historical criticism and literary analysis using methods at first spurned by new approaches but essential to them.

So my principle conclusion would be that the two movements we have discussed so far, have not really been the attacks on biblical criticism that they purported to be, but rather they are parasitic upon it. One thing they do teach us is that texts cannot be confined to their original meaning. But they cannot short-circuit the processes involved in trying to determine what a statement refers to, or the social and cultural context and the many over- or under-tones that provides, or indeed the analysis of sources, the development of the tradition and the reinterpretation of texts in new contexts. It is probably true that one reason why biblical criticism seems to have run into the sand is that so far from producing 'assured results', it throws up one competing hypothesis after another, with no hope or probability of deciding between them, but even if we cannot produce assured results, we can surely maintain the point that the questions remain important and valid even if we are unsure of the answers.

Quite apart from these developments within the area of Biblical Studies itself, there has been a demand for postcritical readings of scripture from literary and theological circles. This has been fired by the hermeneutical concern that the

---

1. See Michael Fishbane, *Biblical Interpretation in Ancient Israel*, OUP, 1985.

deliberate 'distancing' from the text which is vital in the endeavour to discover its strangeness and its meaning in a different world from our own, seems to make it irrelevant. People go on reading the Bible and using it in churches, yet the experts talk about hermeneutical gaps. Should we not feel worried that even at the popular level, the truth of the Bible is thought to be proved by archaeology rather than prayer and action? All great literature transcends its time, and every reader brings much to the reading of any text. There is bound to be a subjective element. The text is not tied to history but has a life of its own. All these seem valid points. But they can encourage an over-simple fundamentalism. If the Bible is to address us, rather than being conformed to our preconceived ideas, it is vital to step back and try to be objective, to distance ourselves and our concerns, and hear what texts have to say that do not fit comfortably into our world. It is appropriate that we do not give in to subjective and partisan readings of the Bible, but endeavour to take seriously the public and objective character of its language. The only way to do this is through the disciplined use of the philological method.

And yet that is not the end of the story. To understand a text it is necessary to know what it refers to. The Bible does not just refer to particular events, or people, or things of the past. It refers to other realities, which it takes to be realities: God, covenant, atonement, worship . . . Can these be dismissed as belonging to that culture? Is it enough to discuss ancient vassal treaties? Could it not be that the dissatisfaction with biblical criticism is not really dissatisfaction with its methods, but with its apparent results? And could not its apparent results be the outcome of limiting the questions to concrete realities we think we can call 'facts'? Why are there so many books about the opponents of Paul when that is not actually what 2 Corinthians is about? It would help us to understand the text if we knew who they were, but there is a lot we can read intelligently without knowing. The crucial questions are what was Paul talking about, and is what he says meaningful and true. Is it true that the God who raised Christ from the dead is the God of all 'comfort' – though here we immediately come up against the cross-cultural and linguistic points already stressed, because 'comfort' simply cannot convey in English all that it would appear to mean in Greek . . .

The heart of the problem is not methodological but theological. For developments within the critical tradition have themselves undermined 'performance' of scripture in terms of 'progressive revelation' or as 'witness' to events behind the text which are really to be identified as the locus of revelation. The primacy of 'history' has become problematic: the Word of God surely cannot be located in those inaccessible events, whose reconstruction is problematic. But if it is located in the words of scripture, then those words turn out to be tied to human cultural constructs and subject to constant reshaping into multiple 'meanings'. The marriage of structuralist and historical approaches leaves us still to grapple with the theological problem of how these literary texts can be treated as Holy Scripture.

But for the moment our conclusion is that no matter how uncertain the conclusions, no matter how difficult it may be to be objective, no matter how much we recognise the validity of a multi-layered approach to interpretation, and accept the fact that the Bible is not tied to its historical origins, the process of biblical criticism remains vital to the enterprise of interpretation, and it must have a future.

In the autumn of 1986 I saw the Stratford production of *Romeo and Juliet*. It was performed in modern dress, there were motor bikes and even a flashy car on stage, Montagues and Capulets were rival street gangs. The text was Shakespeare, but the interpretation had taken a leaf out of *West Side Story*. Having grown up on 'authentic' period costume film productions of Shakespeare, I found at first that the cultural clash between the language of the text and the style of production was too sharp to be meaningful. But by the end of the evening, the sense of a 'timeless' drama in which one was entirely caught up, superseded every other reaction. And in any case how could those film versions be 'authentic'? Shakespeare was originally performed on an Elizabethan apron stage with theatrical conventions long dead. This kind of experience sharpens up the questions about 'authentic' interpretation, and the place of historical research and reconstruction in performance.

This book is an attempt to explore what might be involved in a theology of Holy Scripture, and the issues already raised in this chapter point to the fact that the problems of 'authentic performance' of classics on stage, film or in concert hall are somewhat parallel to discussions about valid interpretation of the Bible.[1] The thesis of this book is that such tensions can be contained within the context of Christian Doctrine as a whole, so as to become coherent with the theological landscape of Christianity. Furthermore, this can be best illuminated by the history of Christian theological use of scripture, particularly in the formative patristic period. The rise of biblical criticism, by drawing attention to the concrete and messy circumstances in which the Bible came to be, in fact enables us to develop a true 'Two Natures' or 'sacramental' view of the Bible, a view not only consistent with other aspects of Christian theology but embryonically present from the beginning, even if its potential was not earlier evident or explicit. In other words, within Christian Theology, the Bible only holds its rightful place if we acknowledge that it is both the Word of God and human words, if we take full account of biblical criticism and the doctrinal concerns underlying fundamentalism. It only comes alive if we face the complex challenges involved in seeking authenticity in performance.

So we might say: "our Holy Scripture is to us one and the same Word, the selfsame perfect in divine inspiration, the selfsame perfect in human utterance, truly of God and truly of Man, one and the same Word, acknowledged in two natures unconfusedly, unchangeably, indivisibly, inseparably, the difference of the natures being in no way removed because of the union, but rather the property of each nature being

1. This analogy has been used independently by Nicholas Lash, 'Performing the Scriptures' in *Theology on the Way to Emmaus*, SCM, 1986; and Brian Jenner, 'Music to the Sinner's Ear?', *Epworth Review*, xvi (1989), pp. 35–8. Each of us develops it in our own way, but clearly a number of points overlap.

preserved and both concurring in the One Word, not as though it were severed or divided into Two Words, but One and the Selfsame Word of God".

Now given modern criticisms of Chalcedonian Christology, it might seem foolhardy to try and adapt such a definition to another area of Christian theology in this way. But for some time, the validity of those criticisms has seemed to the present writer less than apposite, for so far from being hampered by 'outdated substance language', the Definition is concerned with the issue that cannot but lie at the very heart of the matter, namely what an entity – in that case, Christ – really is. In the parallel case of the Bible, an extended metaphor or analogy, that of music and its performance, may help to indicate in what way the 'Two Natures' definition is being understood and adapted.

It is of the essence of music that it is a 'language' embodied in physical reality, and yet an analytical account of sound-waves in the air, resonances and intervals, vibrating strings, reeds or membranes comes nowhere near providing an 'exegesis' of it. Music moves through time, change and development, rhythm as well as melody, being of its essence; yet paradoxically we may speak of time standing still or of experiencing 'timelessness' when caught up in its 'higher' or 'deeper' reality. This 'spiritual nature' is incarnate in a medium of which 'physics' can give an account both explanatory and necessarily reductive, yet it is not translatable into any other medium, except by way of analogy: what music 'means' cannot be expressed in words without change and loss. In order to communicate, music has to be 'realised' through performance and interpretation. Even a silent 'reading' of a score presupposes the possibility of physical sound. Music is 'in Two Natures'.

Through the medium of this 'language', a composer may express more than he consciously 'means' or 'intends' – what Michael Tippett says about *A Child of our Time* only partially conveys the depth of its prophetic insight and power. But the 'performer' or 'interpreter' needs to be able to analyse the material and bring to consciousness what is there if the 'meaning' is to be communicated through the performance. Critical analysis, and the ability to explain the reasons for interpretative decisions, justifies the particular performance. No two performances are identical, and the response of the audience affects the outcome in ways which are not easy to define; this is the common experience of an artist like Janet Baker. Structure and cultural convention, like changes of key and the sequences of cadences, indicate a sense of transition, of development or recapitulation, or of 'ending'. Expectations thus induced are precisely what allows Haydn to surprise, as in the last movement of his Symphony no. 90 in C which purports to end twice before actually doing so. Musician and listener learn a shared communication system, but both have to transcend it: the performer needs to be more than technically competent, and the hearer has to respond by attending to and being taken up into what is happening. In other words both need inspiration.

It is not true that anything goes. A bad performance can be distinguished from a good one. A performance may be professional but wooden (*déjà vu*); or it may be amateur, enthusiastic and winning. Neither is the same as the transcendent subtlety achieved by a genuine 'master'. The amateur player will appreciate far more of that master performance than someone who has never tried. The amateur belongs to the scene, and there would be no 'mastery' if there were not far more less competent devotees, having a go and maintaining interest, ready to hear the 'deeper' subtleties of the truly inspired performance. For such a performance there has to be a sense of 'occasion', a moment of truth for which the performer has been long preparing, and which the audience greets with expectation, ready for a 'revelation', a new awareness of the meaning inherent in the score and awaiting realisation. Such moments of truth usually only arise in the context of a well-known classic, utterly familiar yet strangely renewed. So performance requires a classic and familiar repertoire, though not necessarily a static and closed one.

Music is both culturally conditioned, its conventions, harmonies, rhythms and style being recognisably attributable to particular places and historical periods, and also able to transcend its particularity. Elizabethan music can be 'realised' on modern instruments, and Japanese masters like Suzuki teach Europeans to play instruments of European origin. Contemporary music may have a lasting impact or may 'die'. Much music consists of clichés, repetition and monotonous repetitive rhythm: it feeds passing moods, but has no deeper significance, and is culturally confined. Yet mysteriously, and despite its cultural 'incarnation', music is a universal language, as the greatest artists of the world kept saying on the TV programme *Musicians for Armenia*: even transient music can speak universally, as international festivals like the Nelson Mandela concert demonstrate. Music can communicate and unite across the divides of place and time.

The question is: what is 'authentic' performance of the classics of the past? Does it mean reconstructing instruments at the level of technology available in the composer's time, reducing the size of orchestras, reverting to obsolete playing styles? Does it mean doing painstaking research into precisely what the composer meant by what he wrote? Does it mean unearthing the earliest traceable version, comparing manuscripts, inserting contemporary conventions of harmony or ornamentation? Or does it mean taking advantage of modern technology to produce a sound quite different from anything the composer could have imagined, but which might have delighted his ear? Does it mean 'realising' the music in modern dress so as to communicate its 'deeper' quality to a modern audience?

Debate over this issue parallels debate over biblical interpretation. A performance of Handel's *Messiah* that 'marries' the two extremes may be a 'great' performance, belying the need to settle the methodological debate. The use of harpsichord and countertenor, the insertion of eighteenth-century ornament, alongside a massed choir, proves not to be 'merely academic' or 'archaeological' or inappropriate, but brings a freshness to the performance which gives it new life. Musicology, critical research, enhances a masterly performance. But an 'authentic' performance without inspiration would be as dead as any other bad artistry. The good performance requires respect for the 'medium', with all its constraints and its possibilities, but is impossible without some sense of two co-existing natures, neither of which can 'be' without the other.

The Biblical Canon, then, is as it were the repertoire, inherited, given, to be performed. Selections are performed day by day and week by week in the liturgy. Exegetes, like musicians, need the discipline of rehearsing the score, trying out ways of interpretation, researching the possibilities of meaning, grappling with the 'physical' or 'historical' constraints of the language, preparing for performance with appropriate ornamentation. Without their work, there will be bad performances and false interpretations. Only that kind of work can produce 'masters' like A. S. Peake. But all preachers and congregations are the performers and the hearers on whose inspiration the communication of the Word of God depends. That Word is both 'incarnate' in a time-bound text and yet eternal, transcending the limits of human language and culture. Amateurs and professionals have a go with varying degrees of skill, fostering an audience which will be able to recognise the truly masterly performance. But any good performance has an authenticity of its own.

2

Determining the Canon

Whether we speak of music or drama, we may note that one characteristic of a classic repertoire is the fact that it encompasses a variety of genres: symphonies, concertos, tone poems, opera, comedy, tragedy, satire ... If we pursue our analogy, it is clear that the canon of scripture likewise encompasses a range of genres – it is a kind of classic repertoire. It is fundamentally a library, or collection of books, a fact much clearer to the ancients who would read it from many rolls or codices: it was not then practicable to bind the whole Bible together in one volume. Being a library, not surprisingly it contained books of different types.

Appropriate criteria for authentic performance vary from genre to genre. If it is inappropriate to play Mozart in the same style as the Nineteenth-Century Romantics,[1] it is also inappropriate to play a sonata in the same style as a concerto, or vice versa. Observing differences within the classic repertoire or canon must play a crucial role in interpretation. As already suggested, biblical criticism has had a vitally important contribution to make at this point.

The tendency has been to subsume the whole canon under one genre. Jewish interpretation with its concern for Law has tended to turn all kinds of material, including the narratives of Torah, into legal texts. Early Christian exegesis, though abstracting certain moral prescriptions, rejected the legal interpretation of the scriptures inherited from Judaism, and substituted for it another all-encompassing assumption about

1. See Brian Jenner, 'Music to the Sinner's Ear?' *Epworth Review*, xvi (1989), p. 35.

the genre of scripture, namely that it was prophecy, and not unlike the 'riddling' prophecies of the well-known oracles of the Hellenistic world. As time went on, and for Christians the canon expanded to include the New Testament, the Church interpreted the Bible as a textbook of doctrine, truths revealed for edification and correct belief. The consequent assumption that the Bible is a book of propositions or facts has coloured much debate about its historical character, even as narrative has come to dominate modern perception of its true genre. This trend shares the same danger of reducing the range of genres in the library to one, and thereby distorting performance.

Taking the analogy with a classic repertoire, we can see that it is not necessary for 'canonisation' to remove diversity. The canon does not and need not consist of one definitive composition in one genre. Awareness of the Bible as a canon of literature, representing different styles from different periods, must be the starting-point for appropriate interpretation. Each genre within the Bible will have its proper mode of performance. Narrative, poetry, prophecy, law, wisdom, hymns, prayers, visions – all these require different approaches.

There is, of course, much narrative, some of it in the guise of historical report but not all. To 'perform' narrative appropriately involves retelling the story for the immediate audience. One of the results of biblical criticism has been the discernment of developing narratives, of the process whereby stories were retold even as the biblical texts were formed. There is an inevitable need to 'replay' the stories in different contexts, and in practice this is precisely what has happened in the interpretation of biblical narrative down the centuries. Abraham, Moses, Job, and other great narrative characters of the biblical collection, emerge in the homilies and panegyrics of the Fourth-Century Greek Fathers as exemplary heroes or philosophers, and the stories and characters reappear in Negro spirituals in a very different dress. Preaching has always involved re-telling the stories in one's own words, and all kinds of details are missed out or woven into the narrative, sometimes deliberately, sometimes

27

unconsciously. Appropriate performance does not involve a slavish sticking to the letter of the text, but rather discerning the thrust of the narrative so that it can faithfully be reproduced in a different style with different detail.

It is not for nothing that biblical narrative has been exploited time and time again, alongside other material such as Greek myths, in the imaginative literature and dramatic writing of European culture, including opera. The recent novel by Joseph Heller, *God Knows*,[1] is a fascinating retelling of the story of David, faithful to the stories of the Bible, particularly noting the 'cover-up' job in Chronicles' version compared with the honesty of the narratives in the books of Samuel and Kings, yet transmuted by its style and language, by its 'reading between the lines', into a humorous expression of the scepticism and over-sexed humanity of Twentieth-Century self-consciousness – a brilliant piece of secular interpretation, funny not least because of its bare-faced anachronisms, yet not so secular since it owes much to the Jewish tradition of irreverent story-telling against both oneself and God. This is, at least in part, what *midrash* is all about, and to exclude such imaginative use of scripture on dogmatic grounds is to elevate the letter over the spirit.

But does this mean an absolutely free rein? Or are there criteria limiting the range of appropriate performance? Why do so many people object when this kind of novelistic treatment is given to Jesus, as in Kazantzakis' novel, *The Last Temptation*?[2] What is the relationship between this kind of retelling and distortion? Conversely, was it a kind of 'canonisation' that encouraged the suppression of the more scandalous features of the narratives by the author of Chronicles, just as 'respectability' expurgated Shakespeare? Do we need a kind of 'anti-canonical' interpretation for the canonical literature to be read in its fullness? To such questions we must return, but let us note initially that narrative requires imaginative and creative 'replay'. Attachment to the text and the text

1. Cape, 1984.
2. ET Faber, 1961; the film version produced in the 1980s created more stir than the original book.

alone, or exegesis which is not itself a fresh telling of the narrative, cannot do it justice.

Poetry is another matter. The very nature of poetry lies in its precise wording, its carefully wrought rhythms, or in the case of Hebrew poetry its parallelisms – for structural characteristics depend on the particular cultural conventions within which it is composed. Translating poetry from one language to another is notoriously difficult, largely for this reason. It imposes on the translator an exacting discipline and a creativity equal to that of the original author. Carefree 'putting it into your own words' can never do justice to the demands of poetry. When the 'expert' has endeavoured to translate it, what more can be done by the average 'performer', the reader in church say, than simply read it?

But no – that is not sufficient. Poetry always seems to have layers of meaning, and although teasing them out can sometimes be as crass as explaining a joke, there is always room for discussion and insight, the endeavour to discern the deeper levels of meaning. The reading of poetry is much enhanced when a performer has struggled with how best to do it, to get the tone of voice right, the pace, the shades of meaning into the expression.

And how about law? Law requires application. Since the general principles of law have to be applied to specific cases, and since specific cases envisaged in legal texts are not always exact precedents, and since societies change and their body of law develops, there is a constant process of reinterpretation and reapplication – under the American Constitution, the function of the Supreme Court is to issue authoritative rulings on this process when the matter is in doubt. The body of law found in the Bible was once the actual law of an actual society, and was subject to this process of accretion. Often the layers can be discerned. It was codified as the Torah was gradually put together.

But as this was happening it ceased to be purely legislation for a state and began to become religious law, distinct from the laws operated by the states to which the Jewish people were subject. By processes of interpretation typical of law, it was reapplied to provide moral and practical guidance for

the conduct of daily life according to God's will. In rejecting
the legal interpretation of the Jews, Christians posed real
problems about appropriate performance of legal texts, and
their traditional approach has been piecemeal and inconsist-
ent. Are Seventh Day Adventists right to go back to a literal
reading of the Sabbath commandment? Or is Christian reapplication and reinterpretation legitimate? Whatever the
response to that question, it is not immediately obvious that
it was appropriate to treat legal texts as if they were prophetic
texts as the early church insisted upon doing.

Prophetic texts themselves create problems. Are they cor-
rectly understood as predictive? Biblical criticism has suggested that the traditional Christian reading which has taken
the texts piecemeal and often through allegory found applications to Christ, has failed to produce an appropriate performance. The Israelite prophets, it is often said, forthtold
rather than foretold. The prophetic tradition in Israel, set in
its historical context, is seen as a kind of critical commentary
on Israelite society for its failure to keep God's covenant, the
apparent predictions being warnings of what will inevitably
happen if reform does not take place. Sometimes the prophets
have been seen as the great thinkers of Israel who led the
way to monotheism. But is this simply to confine prophetic
texts to a significance in the past? What would appropriate
contemporary performance be? It is sometimes assumed that
a relevant prophetic critique of the contemporary scene would
meet the requirements. But who has the discernment? And
what role does the canonical text play in this modern re-
enactment? How true is this to the prophetic texts as a whole?
The related genre, apocalyptic, poses further questions, such
as whether visions should be searched for precise predictions,
and whether there can be a re-birth of images and symbols
in a new culture.

Wisdom texts also demand careful consideration. Some
proverbs have simply come over into our own stock of traditional sayings, and some reflections on life and its transitori-
ness have an immediate impact when read in any culture or
century. But so much is confined to the 'wisdom' of a bygone
civilisation, so many assumptions are no longer tenable, so

many of the ordinary conditions of life so different. So while some proverbs may remain fixed and retain their sharpness, others die, or only live by becoming metaphorical. And the proper performance of ancient cosmology is more problematic than dressing the essentials of Job's debate with his comforters in modern analogies. Parables, however, retain their challenging and teasing quality remarkably well, despite the foreign dress: they lose out only when heavily moralised or explained.

But whatever the difficulties, the essential point is made: there is no one proper mode of interpretative performance because the variety of genres demands a variety of styles. The repertoire not only contains the work of many centuries, but the variegated work of many different social groups, with different roles, writing different types of texts, and this diversity has to be respected. It should be an enrichment. A concert made up of only overtures would never seem to get off the ground!

So how does a classic repertoire, with all its variety, emerge? There has been some discussion in recent work about how to define a classic, but there seems little need to get too involved in that. For practical purposes the classic repertoire in drama or music consists of those works which a community of people keep having re-performed. Such works are those judged to have a significance more than merely transient. A somewhat mysterious sifting process takes place. Often the innovatory character of new works provokes their rejection at first, public response tending to favour the merely conventional. But classic works emerge and consolidate their position as lasting, sometimes long after the lifetime of author or composer. Fashionable works, on the other hand, frequently die, but not always. Works may be 'decanonised' or 'recanonised' – the artistic canon is never finally closed.[1]

1. T. S. Eliot, 'What is a classic?', Presidential Address to the Virgil Society in 1944, republished in *On Poetry and Poets*, Faber, 1957, tried to define classics in terms of their inherent qualities. Within the field of English studies, F. R. Leavis and Frank Kermode have kept the discussion going. Poststructuralist developments which challenge the idea that a text has any inherent 'meaning' or 'quality' called the traditional approach into

Where does responsibility lie for the rediscovery of lost classics, for the marginalisation of some works and the canonisation of others? Debates among critics, researches by 'scholars', choices made by directors and programmers, all these contribute in some measure, as does the preference of performers. But audience reaction is also a powerful force, and scholars and critics can be overruled by popular consensus. The problems of distinguishing between mere fashion and genuine survivability are compounded by the role of the audience. And between all these contributors, classics may get lost for a while, and re-emerge as the tastes of the generations are modified. The process is a community one, and ultimate responsibility is difficult to assign. Works which become classics are accorded authority by the community, but do so because they seem to have an authority of their own. Often this is difficult to analyse or explain: there is a self-authenticating quality about this authority, and it is not easy to spell out criteria for inclusion or exclusion.

Some may feel that the implied analogy with the emergence of scripture should not be pressed: circumstances are too

---

question, and more recently the 'canon' of English literature has been attacked as the 'syllabus' of bourgeois education: see e.g. *Re-reading English*, ed. Peter Widdowson, Methuen, 1982. That kind of charge could also be brought against the classical repertoire of concert-hall or theatre, since there too there has been a tendency to exclude popular forms of music and drama. On the other hand, popular music often influences music which aims to be classical, and classics may emerge from popular genres, as in the case of jazz. What is recognised as classical appears to operate within a cultural tradition, building up 'references' or 'allusions', or reacting against them, and the fundamental distinction would appear to be between the transient and the lasting. The concept of the 'classic' has been explored by David Tracy, *The Analogical Imagination: Christian Theology and the Culture of Pluralism*, New York, Crossroad, 1981, and is discussed by Werner G. Jeanrond in *Text and Interpretation as Categories of Theological Thinking*, Gill and Macmillan, 1988. Within theology, the catalyst of the discussion has been the hermeneutics of Gadamer. Tracy's treatment of classics as the 'resources' of a culture is near to the working-model used in this chapter. There may seem to be a hankering for the 'inherent quality' sought by T. S. Eliot and since recognised to be problematic: the justification would be the necessity of doing justice to the sense that the community does not just accord authority to classics, but recognises it.

different, and the canon of Holy Scripture is of a different character. But if we are to do justice to the nature of scripture we have to take account of the human historical process whereby the canon came to be formed, and to note the important similarities with the process outlined above. It seems that it was not until Athanasius, Patriarch of Alexandria, sent his annual Paschal Letter to announce the date of Easter in 367 and in it specified which books were to be read as scripture, that any prescriptive declaration was made, or a list appeared which was identical with the canon we recognise as authoritative. Yet long before, the concept of a scriptural canon was generally accepted, and a number of writers had produced lists, lists with essentially the same core but variations at the fringes.

Tracing the history of the development of the canon depends largely on identifying scriptural quotations in the writings of the first few centuries, and in detail this cataloguing sometimes appears to be just the kind of boring preoccupation scholars indulge in and students regard as irrelevant. But the process of canon formation is far from insignificant, and it is only through the painstaking attempt to reconstruct that process that the factors at work can be properly traced. The results and the debates about remaining uncertainties are important for our discussion here, even if precise details can be left for the textbooks. One difficulty is deciding what significance to attribute to the fact of quotation, for it could simply mean knowledge of a book, as distinct from a sense of its canonicity as authoritative scripture. But the manner in which quotation is introduced may prove an interesting clue.

Like the writings we now regard as the New Testament, the Christian writings of the first two centuries frequently quote the books of the Jewish scriptures. They quote them to substantiate points they wish to make, clearly regarding them as authoritative, and often using formulaic ways of reference or introduction. Already by the time Ben Sira wrote in the early Second Century BC, the Torah had reached fixed form and was for the Jews the authoritative classic containing the revelation of God's will for his people. It contained the terms of the covenant, and its interpretation ensured the proper practices which would maintain the covenant in being.

It remained classic for the Christian sect, though Jewish legal deductions were increasingly abandoned for an interpretation which treated the texts as belonging to a somewhat different genre: they were foreshadowings, or prophecies of a new covenant now established in Christ, and they derived their authority from the fact that they had been fulfilled and Christ could be read in them. Legal deductions (*halakah*) were abandoned on the grounds that the new covenant prophesied by Jeremiah was to be written on the heart, and the gift of the Spirit meant that God communicated his will direct to each member of the community (in theory, though Paul was not the only one to find it problematic in practice!) In time the eternal validity of moral commandments as an expression of God's will came to be recognised, and different 'levels' of law distinguished. But in the first place, Torah was simply adopted into the repertoire without question, and its unquestioned authority was exploited by careful selection of texts to substantiate the new interpretation Christians like Paul were putting upon it. If for the earliest Christians retaining this heritage from their Jewish past was natural, for Gentile converts also it had its inevitability: ancient culture was dominated by a classic canon of literature which was the basis of education, so it was not an altogether strange proceeding to substitute another classic canon when allegiance was changed; furthermore one of the most convincing apologetic arguments for the truth of Christianity was the proof from fulfilment of prophecy, and that depended on having authoritative texts whose fulfilment could be demonstrated.

Also long before the rise of Christianity, the collection of authoritative prophetic writings had been finalised within the Jewish community. Christians would eventually reorganise the collections of books to make prophecy the climax of what they called the Old Testament, clearly pointing towards the fulfilment in the New Testament. But scripture in the time of Jesus was often referred to as 'the Law and the Prophets', as if these two components constituted the whole. Christian communities clearly adopted these writings as classic too, without questioning their place in the canon, indeed believing that their authority was increased by the fact of their fulfilment. Since the books we think of as historical (Joshua/ Judges/Samuel/Kings) were included in the Five Books of the Prophets, a very large part of what we call the Old Testament became classic for Christianity without debate or question.

But at this time the Jewish canon was not finally closed. Beside the fixed corpus of the Law and the Prophets there were writings given virtually equivalent honour, like the Psalms, or the Books of Wisdom passed down, as they believed, from Solomon. As with any classic repertoire, the edges were blurred, and they would not be clarified until after the parting of the ways. Many of these books Christianity inherited without question, referring to them, quoting them as authoritative and with the same formulae as other scriptural writings. However, in early Christian literature, including the New Testament itself, there are references to scriptures which cannot now be found among the canonical writings, and eventually the Church would canonise rather more texts than the Jewish Rabbis. Only at the time of the Reformation when scholars returned to the Hebrew Bible to which these books did not belong, were such texts treated as 'deuterocanonical' or as the books of the Apocrypha.

So the Christian sect inherited a body of classic literature from its parent community, and characteristically the decisions about what belonged were neither final, nor clearly attributable. A complex process of the emergence of a community mind, guided by its scholars the scribes, had undoubtedly been behind this. Some, like the Sadducees and the Samaritans, would accord authority only to the Torah. The idea of a canon existed, with a fixed authoritative core, but despite the ancients' preference for all things ancient, no criterion such as antiquity had effected closure of that canon.

So gradually in Christian literature we find references made to new writings, gradually we find 'apostolic' writings quoted like scripture, gradually specifically Christian writings join the inherited repertoire. It is an interesting question whether an author like Luke, in telling the story of Jesus and the spread of the *ecclēsia* intended to write 'new scripture' to demonstrate the fulfilment of the old: his adoption of biblical Greek style, and of narrative motifs reminiscent of Old Testament narrative, give the suggestion a certain plausibility. But such a motive does not seem to have operated in the case of other New Testament writers. Rather occasional writings came to be valued as 'classic', often because of their association with apostolic figures. And as time went on, their place in Christian 'performance' became established through an emerging consensus. The analogy with the emergence of a classic repertoire is surprisingly close, and the shared life and culture of a community has a crucial role, the details of which cannot be precisely documented.

But so does the influence of 'critics' and 'scholars', 'scribes' or 'bishops'. Popular usage allowed the circulation of many supposedly apostolic books, some Gospels, some epistles, some apocalypses, some 'Acts', and clearly these were at times highly 'fashionable'. So as Christian 'classics' began to emerge with an authority commensurate with the inherited repertoire, distinctions had to be drawn. There was bound to be a movement towards an agreed canon, and consequent pressure in the direction of 'closing' it. Inevitably the authority figures and the scholars would play an important role in deciding what was 'reliable'. Two Second-Century controversies would seem to have had a formative effect in this regard, but the extent to which they were determinative is a matter of some debate in modern scholarship. Probably the questions are unanswerable simply because precision in measuring the relative weight of scholarly argument and popular consensus, perhaps virtually inarticulate, is as elusive here as in the formation of any other classic repertoire. What the 'scholars' said was only effective because it was recognised as cohering with community instincts and community practice.

Still an outline of these ancient controversies, and a clarification of the issues subject to debate, will help us to understand the process of canonisation, and to determine what criteria, if any, were in operation. The first key figure is Marcion. What he advocated is only known to us through the opposition since his works were suppressed and are lost, but in a sense the reaction of the opposition is more important for our purposes than the 'historical Marcion'.

Irenaeus, bishop of Lyons, wrote a large work *Against the Heresies*[1] towards the end of the Second Century. In this book a number of references are made to Marcion, but Irenaeus promises to write a special book against this particular heretic, a promise he apparently never redeemed, though the promise is itself an indication that for all their similarities, he recognised a difference between Marcion and the Gnostics he was then engaged in refuting: Marcion "is the only man who has dared openly to mutilate the scriptures," he explains, "and unblushingly above all others to inveigh against God".

So in Book I.27.2, he mentions Marcion's

> most daring blasphemy against Him who was proclaimed as God by the law and the prophets, declaring that he was the cause of evils, desirous of war, changeable in opinion and the author of inconsistent statements. He says that Jesus came from the Father, who is above the Creator . . . that he rendered null and void the prophets and the law and all the works of the Creator God . . . He used an expurgated edition of the Gospel of Luke, removing all the passages that referred to the birth of our Lord, and many things from his teaching in which he plainly referred to the Creator of the universe as his Father. In the same way he mutilated the Epistles of Paul, cutting out all that the Apostle said about the God who made the world, and which went to show that he was the Father of our Lord Jesus Christ, and also passages bearing on the advent of our Lord which that Apostle had quoted from the prophets.

We know that Justin Martyr wrote against Marcion earlier in the century, and that Marcion was his contemporary. Later Tertullian, the first Christian to write in Latin, would devote an enormous work to refuting Marcion, and he frequently quoted from Marcion's writings in order to do so.[2] The

1. The text was edited by W. W. Harvey, 2 vols, CUP, 1857: a translation will be found in the *Ante-Nicene Christian Library*, Edinburgh, 1868.
2. Text ed. and tr. Ernest Evans, 2 vols, OUP, 1972.

Marcionite 'denomination' survived for several centuries. But the summary quoted from Irenaeus lays out the essential points of his doctrine as they affect our subject. Whether Marcion was basically a Gnostic, or an extreme follower of Paul, like him rejecting the Law for the Gospel, we need not decide. We may note, however, an implied contrast between the God of wrath found in the Jewish scriptures and the loving Father of Jesus Christ, a point tackled later by Irenaeus with careful exegetical proofs from the writings Marcion himself accepted. Marcion anticipated the moral difficulties some modern liberal Christians have with the Old Testament. And on these grounds, he rejected those scriptures as coming from a different God, replacing them with selected Christian documents.

Now the crucial issue in relation to the formation of the canon is whether the word 'replace' is appropriate. Did Marcion dream up the idea of a Christian canon to replace the canon of the Jewish scriptures which was the only one in use in the Church? Or was the 'New Testament' (as yet unnamed) already emerging, so that he modified an already existing list? If the answer 'Yes' is given to the first of those questions, then a second emerges: did Irenaeus, in reaction both against Marcion and against heretics who treated the scriptures piecemeal, essentially adopt Marcion's idea of 'new scripture'? Was he an innovator in propounding the idea of an apostolic canon alongside the canon of the Jewish scriptures, as von Campenhausen has suggested?[1]

There is much to be said for von Campenhausen's view: the mere proliferation of Christian books in the Second Century suggests that as yet there was no strong sense of anything special about certain texts, and although writers like Justin refer to 'memoirs of the apostles' being read in worship, there is little to suggest that knowledge of such books implied their canonisation on a level with the Jewish scriptures. It is in the works of Irenaeus that we find for the first time a defence of the fourfold Gospel alongside a collection of Pauline epistles, an organisation of texts somewhat parallel to the fivefold

---

1. *The Formation of the Christian Bible*, ET Fortress, 1972.

collections of the law and the prophets. Irenaeus' list does not exactly correspond with the list eventually fixed, or even with other near-contemporary lists, but as in the case of the Jewish canon, the core is fixed, and authority is accorded to it.

Irenaeus still speaks of old and new covenant in a general way rather than as a way of specifically referring to collections known as the Old Testament and the New Testament, but his contrast between the prophetic writings and the apostolic writings indicates that the concept is there in embryo if not the terminology. He certainly groups the core Christian writings with the Jewish scriptures referring to them without differentiation as the 'scriptures of the Lord'. He keeps insisting that the apostles, the prophets and the Lord himself consistently teach what he is advancing: and this phraseology seems to refer to the apostolic witness in both Gospels and epistles, the Jewish scriptures and the teaching of Jesus as recorded in the Gospels. So his defence of the unity of the scriptures, both old and new, against the views of Marcion and against the piecemeal selection and interpretation of the Gnostics, establishes a 'Bible' for the first time. There seems to be no denying his crucial contribution.

And yet the fundamental appeal of Irenaeus is to tradition in the Church, particularly as embodied in the apostolic succession from Peter in Rome. This is contrasted with the esoteric traditions of the Gnostic groups as being public, open, and universal. The teaching of the Church is constant and abiding, and supported by the testimony of prophets, apostles and all the disciples, he asserts. One suspects that the 'systematisation' and justification may originate from Irenaeus, but his own position would be profoundly undercut if his conclusions did not resonate with an emerging consensus, if the 'audience' did not recognise a statement of its own unarticulated views about the classic repertoire. And in fact von Campenhausen recognises that the idea of the New Testament canon, once enunciated, quickly caught on precisely for this reason. It may not be possible to decide whether earlier Marcion modified such an emerging canon, or alternatively chose from certain books in popular use to produce a substitute for the existing canon of the Jewish scriptures alone, thereby becoming the creator of the idea of a Christian canon. What is certain is that he precipitated the rapid crystallisation of a consensus that may have been slowly forming, and provoked the explicit recognition of the New Testament as a collection to take its place alongside the Old – eventually indeed to provide the standards by which the Old would be interpreted.

The other Second-Century controversy certainly hastened the closure of that canon once the idea of it began to spread. Again we are dependent largely on opponents for reports and the 'historical Montanus' is elusive. It could be that the Montanist movement was merely an outbreak of charismatic and eschatological fervour. Most reports suggest that Montanists were orthodox in doctrine, and concentrate on their 'false prophecy' and the absurdity of thinking a town in Asia Minor would be the heavenly city. But some suggest that Montanus claimed to be the incarnation of the Paraclete, and one reported saying of his suggests that his understanding of prophecy was influenced by Hellenistic norms: "Behold a man is as a lyre, and I fly over it like a plectrum. The man sleeps and I remain awake. Behold it is the Lord that stirs the hearts of men, and gives men hearts"[1] – the lyre on which the deity plays is a standard Greek analogy and foreign to the biblical tradition.

The so-called 'orthodox' Church groups reacted by distinguishing, justifiably or not, between rational inspiration and irrational ecstasy, and also by becoming chary of "adding another paragraph or clause to the wording of the New Covenant of the Gospel, to which nothing can be added, from which nothing can be taken away", to quote the antimontanist, Apollinarius of Hierapolis.[2] To use newly-inspired books of prophecy in worship was taken to be presumptuous. The 'innumerable books' of the Montanist prophets confuse the minds of those unable to test them, suggest Hippolytus in Third-Century Rome.[3] This is what happens to uninstructed and thoughtless people who do not keep carefully to the

1. Quoted in Epiphanius, *Haer*. 48.4.
2. Extracts preserved by the Church Historian Eusebius, *Hist. Eccles.*, V.16.
3. *Refutation of all Heresies*, VIII.19.1–3.

scriptures, but pay more heed to human traditions, to their own fancies, dreams, inventions and old wives' tales.[1] The principle of closure began to be established, though the precise lists remained pretty flexible at the edges for a long time yet. Apocalypses were very popular in the early church, but Montanism put them all under suspicion, and what we know as the Book of Revelation would not for some centuries be generally accepted as belonging to scripture in much of the East: as late as 692 a Council produced two lists, one with Revelation and one without.

The closing of the canon, a process paralleled in Judaism at about the same period, does not find a parallel in any 'classic repertoire' or literary canon: generally a hard core of classics establishes itself, but as in the early centuries of Christianity, the edges remain blurred. We may guess at the factors producing this unique situation. Firstly, the doctrine of fulfilment so basic to early Christianity meant that there was a finality about the New Covenant which would rub off on the collection of books which came to embody it and bear its title. By the Third Century, Tertullian, even though he became a Montanist, was chary of questioning the concept of a definitive list to which nothing could be added; the Paraclete inspired living prophecy, particularly purity regulations, rather than adding to the scriptures. The New Covenant in Christ was final.

In the second place, the formation into collected 'blocks' such as the fourfold Gospel was stimulated by the need to distinguish which of the many books were a direct record of the apostolic proclamation, and no recent writing could make such a claim. Innovation was associated with the speculations of the Gnostics, and attempts to pass off novel teaching under the names of the apostles reinforced the need to make critical distinctions. It is often suggested that the key criterion for this was apostolicity, but there are some difficulties with this: the Gospels of Mark and Luke were recognisably not written by apostles, and many rejected documents purported to have apostolic authorship. The important factor was probably not

1. *Comm.Dan.*, IV.20.1.

41

apostolic authorship as such, but the presence of recognisably reliable testimony.

How was that to be established? The answer seems to be by assurance of a book's antiquity from the common tradition of its public usage in the Church, and by its coherence with the apostolic teaching passed down in the Church. It is noticeable that Irenaeus had to argue for acceptance of the Gospel of John because of suspicions in some quarters, and while he made a case for apostolic authorship, it was not superfluous to back this up by tracing the line of succession down to himself through Polycarp. Likewise von Campenhausen has argued that the earliest known list of scriptural books, the so-called Muratorian Canon, does not claim apostolic authorship for every text; rather it seeks documents that are ancient and reliable. This interest in antiquity meant that closure was inevitable as the idea of a normative scripture deriving from Christ and his disciples gained ground against competing texts and theories. The common sense of the Church was more important than any specifically articulated criterion for distinguishing what did and did not belong.

The factors producing closure of the canon so far outlined are specific to Christianity, and we have to take cognisance of the fact that the same unusual process was happening in the Jewish schools of the period. Neither religious tradition would in future allow much blurring at the fringes, and the kind of constant flexibility in other 'canons' ceased to be possible. Is there anything in common that provoked this parallel move? We should not perhaps underestimate the effect of the idea that scripture was more than merely human literature, that here were documents having the stamp of God's authority. We cannot view this simplistically: the ancient Greeks believed all literature was inspired by the Muses, and that did not close the literary canon. But long before Christianity had come on to the scene, much of Israel's ancient literature had been formed into the Torah, a defined corpus interpreted as authoritative for living the religious life because it was God-given, and subject not to addition but interpretation. So perhaps the most important factor was the treatment of these texts as not simply containing 'law' but belonging to the genre 'law', thus according to them a more than literary authority, an apartness which became sanctity, an authority with divine sanction, since the law was revealed by God. This authority was transferred to other canonical collections like the prophets, and then the fourfold Gospel . . .

So in a sense there were several 'mini-closures' of the canon along the way, and an overall sense that nothing could be added to a definitive revelation would eventually hallow the ancient 'classics', separating them from all subsequent writing, no matter how 'inspired'. We are left with a rather haphazard human process producing a unique collection of writings which are what they are because paradoxically they are regarded as more than human.

Christian tradition and Christian theology give us the Bible, a unified whole, these days bound in one volume, in a translation which gives it a homogeneous style. History gives us a collection of documents varied in language, style, origin, date, authorship, character, genre, purpose, attitude, theology and so on. To do justice to the Bible we have to retain the element of 'givenness' while 'unimagining' it and taking account of the somewhat messy human business of the canon's formation.

The notion of a classic repertoire allows us to do some justice to this tension. Where a classic repertoire exists, we accept the fact that many different elements went into the writing or composing and preserving of a complex and diverse collection of material, and this is evidently true of the Bible. We also recognise the potential for different and diverse readings of a repertoire – in fact we expect new performances to have an element of novelty, and new readings to see new things in classic texts, and so we do not have the same expectations of unity in the case of 'artistic canons' as Christian tradition has taught us to expect in the case of the Bible. Clearly as 'classics' of world literature, the books of the Bible are open to 'anti-canonical' readings, and just as new performances 're-read' Shakespeare or Beethoven, so there will be 'replays' of biblical material which may or may not accord with the norms of Christian tradition.

Yet a classic repertoire belongs to a community, and is

usually built up by a process of quotation and allusion, development and reaction, implying an underlying continuity, a tradition, a developing 'culture', which provides a kind of 'normativity', and has a certain 'authority'. The existence of specific communities to which the biblical texts 'belong' has created 'normative reading' of the texts, a feature of all 'classical canons' to the extent that they are read or performed for a community and in a tradition. For Christians, the Bible has that kind of 'givenness', and more – for the closure of the canon is related to the fact that some 'readings' have been recognised as inauthentic, as subversive of the text, and to the fact that these documents were recognised as 'more than human'.

For Irenaeus it was vital that the Bible presents a coherent 'testimony' pointing in the same direction, that there was a kind of underlying 'plan' despite the surface variegations. Furthermore, that unity is placed in a theological arena: it is given because the Bible is the Word of God. This unity of the Bible, its importance and the temptations it presents for interpretation, will be examined in the following chapter, which will explore the question what difference it makes that the works in our 'classic repertoire' have to be regarded as parts of a whole? Meanwhile we should note that this chapter's explorations have led us again to the 'Two Natures' issue. To do justice to the Bible, unity must be found incarnated in diversity, and interpretation of God's Word has to take account of what is appropriate to the different genres of a body of literature whose content has been determined by a community process analogous to that whereby any classic repertoire is formed. Justice has to be done to the human historical process, and yet that process itself requires a recognition that these documents have a more than human authority.

3

Tradition and Interpretation

For classic performance, tradition is indispensable. A creative artist will certainly bring something inspired to the job, but an entirely novel performance would not be a rendering of the classic work. Traditions about appropriate speed and dynamics are passed from master (or mistress) to pupil, from one generation to another, and a radical performance will be deliberate reaction against those traditions if it violates them. The accretion of tradition may sometimes need to be challenged: Mozart was not a romantic!

The performance of an individual work not only depends on the tradition of its performance, but also on its place in the classic repertoire. The total corpus of that composer's work will illuminate the direction of his development and knowledge of it will help to 'place' the particular work in question in its proper context, so perhaps affecting its performance. The circumstances of the composer's life at the time of writing may bear on it too. But even more important may be the way it relates to the period in which the composer lived and its place in the development of the artistic tradition – in other words its relationship with the classic repertoire. Schoenberg's music depended upon the need to create a new musical language, a factor produced both by the age in which he lived and the state of the art at the time.

Thus far the analogy again works well when we turn to the question of biblical interpretation. May we press it further? It would appear that the place of a particular work in the repertoire or 'canon' matters, yet it is not determinative of interpretation and the canon cannot itself provide a unitive framework. If that is true of an artistic repertoire, is it true

45

also of the biblical canon? If it is, then canon criticism is in difficulties. A 'repertoire' does not seem able to provide within itself the criteria for interpreting itself. Current literary criticism may speak of a unitive text doing just that: but can the Bible be regarded as a unitive text? There would seem to be considerable dangers in making that assumption, tempting though it is.

But it might be the case that the closure of the biblical canon makes that kind of difference, so that whereas an 'artistic' canon can never be seen as a whole because it is always changing, the Bible in a single volume may be regarded as a unitive text and as such capable of providing its own canons of interpretation. But does it actually do so? Further study of Irenaeus would suggest that it is rather the case that as tradition ensured antiquity and antiquity ensured canonical status, so tradition is the determinative criterion, and tradition rather than the text itself provides the canons of classic performance.

Irenaeus' great work *Against the Heresies*[1] was directed not against Marcion, except by the way, but rather against the Gnostics. In his first book he claims to expose their teachings, and this is what he says about their treatment of the scriptures:

> Such then is their system, which the prophets did not announce, the Lord did not teach, and the Apostles did not hand down; but which they boastfully declare that they understand better than others, reading it in the *Agrapha*. And, as the saying is, they attempt to make ropes of sand in applying the parables of the Lord, or prophetic utterances, or Apostolic statements to their plausible scheme, in order that they may have foundation for it. But they alter the scriptural context and connection, and dismember the truth as much as they can. By their perversions and changes, and by making one thing out of another, they deceive many with their specious adaptations of the oracles

1. References *cit.sup.*

of the Lord. It is just as if there was a beautiful representation of a king made in a mosaic by a skilled artist, and
one altered the arrangement of the pieces of stone into the
shape of a dog or a fox, and then should assert that this
was the original representation of a king. In much the same
manner, they stitch together old wives' tales, and wresting
sayings and parables, however they may, from the context,
attempt to fit the oracles of God into their myths. (*Adv.
Haer.* I.8.1)

A little later on Irenaeus refers to the custom of composing
'centos' of Homer: selected lines were taken out of context
and strung together to make a new poem – a very clever
scholarly hobby! But as Irenaeus points out (I.9.4), "anyone
who knew Homer would recognise the lines but not accept
the story".

What then is the remedy? Of course Irenaeus argues over
and over again for the unity of the scriptures, and also, given
the views of both Marcion and the Gnostics, for the unity of
the one God from whom the scriptures derive. But he is aware
that the scriptures could not provide their own canons of
interpretation, even if there were agreement as to what constituted the scriptures – which, as we have seen, there was not.
There has to be some overarching sense of what the scriptures
are about, some framework which allows the interpreter to
fit the pieces of mosaic together in the appropriate way.

Now 'anyone who knew Homer' would make these judgments from context. The text itself provides the 'overarching
story' with which the reader is familiar. Why the need of a
framework, apart from the reader's memory? Of course context does to some extent suffice – it is easy for Irenaeus to
argue that the one subject of the Johannine Prologue should
not be divided into a multiplicity of subjects, which is what
Gnostics did when they found there all their pleroma of aeons
with their various titles: Monogenes (Only-Begotten), Arche
(First Principle=Beginning), Soter (Saviour), Logos (Word),
Christ, Zoe (Life), Phos (Light), and so on. The immediate
context could indeed be used to exclude some of their false
interpretations, but Irenaeus sensed that immediate context

was not enough, and that overall context would be unclear to an undirected reader put in a library with a pile of codices. Disputes about the contents of scripture, disputes about the reference of prophetic texts and about the status of the Jewish law, alerted him to the fact the scriptures were not self-sufficient, the reader not competent without instruction to construct a coherent view of their direction. Interpreters needed the guidance of an overall framework, and that overall framework was provided by a community which understood the unitive story to which the diverse documents gave testimony, and had a tradition of appropriate performance of the text.

For Irenaeus this framework was enshrined in the Rule of Faith or the Canon of Truth.

> Anyone who knew Homer [he suggested] would recognise the verses (meaning lines), but not accept the story. In the same way he who has the Rule of Truth steadfast in himself, which he received at his baptism, will recognise the scriptural names, quotations, parables, but will not accept their blasphemous system as scriptural. For even though he may know the stories, he will not take the fox's portrait for the king's. But referring each quotation to its own context, and its own place in the body of truth, he will expose and refute their theory. (*Adv. Haer.* I.9.4)

To what was Irenaeus referring when he spoke of the Rule of Truth? For a long time it was assumed that it was the Apostles' Creed, but critical scholarship now recognises that there are no grounds for the assumption that a creed as such was known at the end of the Second Century.[1] In the Fourth Century we meet what is known as the Old Roman Creed, which is clearly the ancestor of the Apostles' Creed but not identical with it. We also find attached to it[2] the legend that the apostles got together to agree this brief summary of the faith before scattering all over the place to preach the Gospel,

1. The classic treatment of the history of the creeds is J. N. D. Kelly, *Early Christian Creeds*, Longmans, 1960.
2. In the works of Rufinus, *Comm. in symb. apost.* 2.

intending thus to ensure the unity and coherence of the faith everywhere. So in the Fourth Century the Old Roman Creed must have been sufficiently established to be regarded as ancient and traditional. In that period, however, every local church seems to have its own creed, and while these creeds follow a similar shape they are not identical. They clearly arose in the context of training for baptism, the creed becoming the standard way of ensuring that converts knew by heart a summary of Christian belief. Reference to such memorised creeds show that they were often treated as a convenient summary of the scriptures for those incapable of reading them all for whatever reason.[1]

Now Irenaeus' Rule of Truth shares some features with the creeds: it is associated with what a Christian receives at baptism, and it is regarded as a summary of the overarching Christian story contained in scripture. It does not, however, appear to be a fixed formula to be committed to memory. Irenaeus gives us several different versions, and others are found in the works of Tertullian and also the writings of Origen, the great Alexandrian scholar of the Third Century. These various accounts of the Rule of Faith cover the same sort of ground and often contain the same stereotyped phrases, but clearly they reflect a flexible oral tradition rather than the existence of a creed or creeds as such. The importance of the Rule of Truth for Irenaeus is that it outlines the simple orthodox 'system' which alone gives the key to the scriptures and which excludes the fanciful interpretations of the Gnostics. The foundation on which this rests is tradition, and just as the content of the Canon of scripture rested on the public tradition which could be traced back to the apostles, so did the canons of interpretation enshrined in the Rule of Truth.

To what extent can it be said that this Canon of Truth was simply a summary of scripture, a résumé of the 'plot' as it were? Let us turn to examine its content. This is how it appears in the first book *Against the Heresies*, in other words the context we have been discussing:

1. Cyril of Jerusalem, *Cat. Orat.* v.12.

The Church, although scattered over the whole world even to its extremities, received from the Apostles and their disciples the faith in one God, the Father Almighty, Maker of heaven and earth, the seas and all that in them is, and in one Christ Jesus, the Son of God, who became incarnate for our salvation, and in the Holy Spirit, who by the prophets proclaimed the dispensations, the advents, the virgin birth, the passion and resurrection from the dead, the bodily ascension of the well-beloved Christ Jesus our Lord into heaven, and his Parousia from the heavens in the glory of the Father to gather up all things in Himself and to raise the flesh of all mankind to life in order that "everything in heaven and in earth and under the earth should bow the knee" (Phil. 2:10ff) to Christ Jesus our Lord and God, our Saviour and our King, according to the will of the invisible Father and that every tongue should confess to him, and that he should pronounce a just judgment upon all, and dismiss the spirits of wickedness and the angels who transgressed and became apostate, and the ungodly, unrighteous, lawless and profane into everlasting fire, but in his graciousness should confer life and reward of incorruption and eternal glory upon those who have kept his commandments and have abided in his love either from the beginning of their life or from their repentence. (*Adv. Haer.* I.10.1)

What is noticeable is that it is not a summary of the story of the scriptures. Such a summary would begin as this does with God as Creator, but would then outline the Fall, the call of Abraham, the stories of the patriarchs, the descent into Egypt, the Exodus, the entry into the Promised Land, the judges and the kings, the disobedience of Israel and the work of the prophets, the exile, the return, the life of Jesus, the mission of the Church, the vision of the End. As we shall see a bit later on, Irenaeus comes near to providing such an outline in another work, *The Demonstration of the Apostolic Preaching*,[1] but that is certainly not what we have here. The framework for

1. Discovered in Armenia and first published 1907; ET J. A. Robinson, SPCK, 1920.

interpreting the scriptures is an abstract which focuses on key perspectives: the coherence of the activity of God the Creator, his Son Jesus Christ, and the Spirit who inspired the prophecies and predicted the significant features of the Jesus story – his birth, passion, resurrection, ascension and return. The climax is the just judgment of Christ, who is both Saviour and King, and judges according to the will of the Father, and in the description of this enter ideas such as the fall of the angels which have no obvious place in the scriptures which Irenaeus regarded as canonical. The scriptures provide the odd quotation, and the statement is clearly informed by the scriptures, but it is not straightforwardly a summary of them. As noted above, it is not simply a case of knowing the story, and therefore recognising context. The analogy with Homer is not exact.

Let us compare another version, this one appearing some chapters on in the same book of the *Adversus Haereses*:

The Rule of Truth we hold is that there is one God Almighty, who made all things by his Word, and fashioned and formed that which has existence out of that which had none. As the Scripture saith, "By the Word of the Lord and the Spirit of his mouth were the heavens and all their glory established" (Ps. 33:6). And again, "All things were made by Him and without him was not anything made" (John 1:3). There is no exception: but the Father made all things by Him, both visible and invisible, objects of sense and intelligence, temporal, eternal and everlasting. And such He did not make by angels or by any powers separated from His Thought. For God needs nought of such things: but it is He who by His word and Spirit makes, disposes, governs and gives being to all things, who created the universe, who is the God of Abraham, Isaac and Jacob. Above Him there is no other God, neither initial principle, nor power, nor pleroma. He is the Father of our Lord Jesus Christ. Following this Rule we shall easily show that the heretics, in spite of their many and various assertions, have erred from the truth. (*Adv. Haer.* I.22.1)

Again we can hardly claim that we have here a summary of the story of the scriptures. Rather it is an assertion of the doctrine that the God who created the world is the same as the transcendent God, the same as the God of the Jews, and the one who sent the Saviour. In creating he did not need to delegate to any inferior being, but rather acts entirely through his own Word and Spirit. The expression of this doctrine with its concentration on the creative process and its continuity with the process of revelation and salvation, is deliberately geared to excluding the doctrines of Irenaeus' rivals for whom the Creator God could not conceivably be the same as the Ultimate Father. It is assumed to be scriptural and is supported by scriptural quotations, but it provides a theological framework which goes beyond what is explicit or obviously suggested by the bare texts without the benefit of tradition. In wording and content it stands little detailed comparison with the earlier example, though it has a somewhat similar shape and argument.

Different again is the summary of the faith found in Book III. Here Irenaeus introduces it as the truth passed to the Church by the Apostles. It is the tradition of the truth which is to be esteemed, and if there are any doubts about it, enquiry should be made from the oldest churches in which the Apostles lived. This would be so even if the Apostles had not given us the Scriptures, he suggests:

> Many nations of barbarians who believe in Christ and have their salvation not written on paper with ink, but by the Spirit on their hearts, assent to this order, and carefully keep the old tradition, believing in one God the Maker of heaven and earth and of all therein, by Christ Jesus the Son of God. He, on account of his exceeding love for his creation, submitted to the birth from a virgin, and himself through himself uniting man with God, suffered under Pontius Pilate, and rising again was received with splendour. And is to come in glory as Saviour of those who are saved, and Judge of those who are judged, sending to eternal fire those who disfigure the truth and despise his Father and his own incarnation. They who hold this faith without

writing may be barbarians as regards our language, but as regards opinions, habits and way of life are most wise on account of their faith. They also please God, living in all righteousness, pureness and wisdom. (*Adv. Haer.* III.4.1)

One might almost be tempted to think that the scriptures have here become secondary to the apostolic tradition, but looking at Irenaeus' work as a whole, it is clear that scripture is not only part of the tradition handed down from the apostles but essential to it, for the consistent witness of prophets, apostles and Gospel guarantees the tradition, even as tradition establishes both the Canon and the canons of interpretation. Book III in fact begins the assembly of scripture proofs against the heretics, which will be followed by proofs from the words of the Lord and the apostolic letters in Books IV and V. That is the context in which this passage occurs.

So scripture and tradition are inseparable, and it is for that reason that difficulties in scripture are not insuperable, and the unity and harmony of scripture can be discerned. The kernel of scripture, the framework which is partly external to the text yet encapsulates the essential meaning of the text, is enshrined in the plan of salvation, and it was "through those from whom the Gospel came to us that we have learnt the plan of our salvation. For what they preached they afterwards handed down to us by the will of God in the scriptures, to be the foundation and pillar of our faith" (*Adv. Haer.* III.1.1).

Irenaeus found his opponents slippery: for when they were refuted from scripture, they suggested that the books had no authority and only tradition counted, but when they were faced with tradition, they fell back on theories of contamination so that they could be selective, or appealed to esoteric traditions which the apostles conveyed privately to the perfect. In the last resort Irenaeus' only recourse was to pour scorn on the idea that the apostles would have consigned the truth to unknowns and concealed it from the obvious leaders of the Church – the public and universal teaching of the Church was his ultimate appeal. And that deposit included the prophetic and apostolic books, together with the canons of appropriate interpretation. Scripture and tradition were inseparable, the one endorsing the other.

However, faced with the Gnostic menace, Irenaeus had to do more than woodenly replay the scores he had inherited. As we have already seen, he went further than anyone had before in spelling out which books were scriptural, justifying their selection, and arranging them in categories. He was prepared to constitute collections of 'new scriptures' to take their place alongside the old, perhaps taking a leaf out of Marcion's book, certainly articulating a consensus that had probably been long emerging concerning which books belonged to the apostolic tradition because of their antiquity and generally recognised reliability. His activity would ensure a fairly rapid shift of perception, so that the old scriptures were subordinated to the new. But he also had to embark on formulating the first systematic theology. For in showing how the tradition and the biblical text were to be 'performed', he found himself articulating a 'biblical theology', which used ideas current before, but developed them much further in order to spell out that 'plan of salvation' which provided the kernel of the scriptures' unity and coherence.

For the framework which provided the canons of traditional interpretation itself demanded exposition and development: recent discoveries of original Gnostic texts, such as the Nag Hammadi Library, reinforce the view that the emphases of this biblical theology, as well as the particular selection of material in the Rule of Faith, was directly affected by the character of the doctrines Irenaeus was opposing. Tradition could not survive without some innovation, or at least extension and re-expression. Theological thinking as well as tradition had to contribute to the framework within which the Bible was to be interpreted.

The doctrine of 'recapitulation' is the development most often associated with Irenaeus' theology:

> ... as through the disobedience of one man, first to be made of the virgin soil, many were made sinners and lost their life; so it was necessary that by the obedience of one man, first to be born of a virgin, many should be made

righteous and receive salvation. Accordingly the Word became flesh, God *recapitulating* the ancient creation of man in himself, in order to slay sin, to remove death's sting, and restore man to life. (*Adv. Haer.* III.18.7)

Irenaeus himself acknowledges his debt to Justin, who in a work against Marcion (now lost) had asserted that he would not have believed the Lord if he had announced another God beside Our Creator, Maker and Supporter; it was only because he came to us 'recapitulating' God's creature in himself, that his faith remained unshaken. Elsewhere in Justin's writings we find sketched, on the basis of Romans 5, the parallel between Adam and Christ which Irenaeus would elaborate in order to spell out his 'recapitulation' theory.

So in a sense Irenaeus was not an innovator. He finds the 'plan of salvation' in a story of loss and recovery: of Adam the innocent, set in Paradise, foolishly disobedient, not least because of the wiles of an angel who fell from heaven for this misdeed and became Satan; and of Christ, the new Adam, going over the same ground again, but this time being obedient, reversing the process, bringing salvation to humanity. This he abstracts from tradition and sharpens up, elaborating the detailed parallels, between Eve and Mary, the tree of disobedience and the tree of obedience, and so on. This is the 'lynch-pin' of his scheme of scriptural unity, for the old scriptures set the scene of human disobedience and prophesy the remedy, and the new scriptures give testimony to the fulfilment of prophecies and promises. The creative purpose of God was marred, but then restored.

Complete innovation it may not have been, but its new development as an interpretative system was undoubtedly stimulated by the particular claims of Irenaeus' opponents. The recently discovered Gnostic documents[1] have made clear the importance of Genesis in their systems. Gnostics were primarily interested in cosmology, in showing how sparks of spirit had become trapped in a material cosmos, in revealing

1. See *The Nag Hammadi Library in English*, ed. James Robinson, Brill, Leiden, 1977, especially *The Apocryphon of John* and the *Hypostasis of the Archons*.

55

how by self-knowledge spirits might escape and return to the spiritual pleroma. They were generally alienated from the Demiurge, the Creator God who had produced this rotten material world, and spun 'myths and genealogies' to show he was a fallen being. Elements of Genesis were often woven into their cosmological accounts: the Creator was a 'jealous' God, jealous of the higher spiritual principles; the serpent was the embodiment of Wisdom, who brought knowledge of good and evil, so enabling the trapped spirits to escape the clutches of the Demiurge.

How was such an interpretation of Genesis to be met? Did it not have some plausibility: after all, knowledge of good and evil is presumably a good and useful acquisition, and it is difficult to see why the Creator should deprive his creatures of it; and did not Jesus tell people to be 'wise as serpents'? It may not be easy for us to imagine how the text could be turned upside down like that, but there is little in the text itself to exclude such an interpretation if you come to it with a different set of assumptions. Irenaeus not only insisted upon an alternative framework, by appealing to tradition and the Rule of Faith, but also produced a different 'performance' of the story. In doing so he, like his opponents, introduced elements that were not part of the text itself, like the tempting angel, and he too selected those elements in the story that cohered with his 'system'. But that just confirms the point: not only is a framework necessary for interpretation, but a systematic theology also, and both will need to be at the same time traditional and 'novel' to meet the challenge of performing the text in a situation where its traditional meaning is being subverted.

Irenaeus' emphasis on 'recapitulation' undergirded the development of a theology of salvation as re-creation, and this too was focused by its contrast with the claims of his rivals. Gnostics understood the Christ to have revealed to trapped spirits the heavenly world to which they really belonged and the way of escape to it: redemption meant rescue from creation, and the God of creation was opposed to the God of salvation. Irenaeus insists that creation and redemption are not opposite but complementary, shaping the precise content of his Rule of Faith to clarify that point, and systematising a whole range of ideas and images that the Church had used in its preaching into the overarching story of fall and restoration.

Linked with this is his development of Second-Century Logos-theology, the understanding of the pre-existent Christ as the Reason or Thought of God projected forth as his Word, so becoming the instrument of the transcendent Father in creation, revelation and redemption. Irenaeus built this into a Trinitarian view of the one God and his providential activity, picking up the biblical image of the 'two hands' of God, which were identified as the Word and the Spirit. He also saw the continuity between the Logos creating man in God's image, and restoring that image to humanity by himself taking human nature in the incarnation: his comment that 'he became what we are, so that we might become what he is' (*Adv. Haer.* V. praef.) would reverberate through the theology of the subsequent centuries, especially in the work of Athanasius. Redemption meant not escape from the created order, but rather the realisation of God's creative purposes through his own activity in renewing and restoring what he had created.

In affirming creation and new creation, Irenaeus would also stress the boundlessness of the all-encompassing God, who contains all things without himself being contained, and the utter dependence of creation, which he brought into being out of nothing, on his sovereign will. Both ideas had some precedent, but Justin, Irenaeus' predecessor in so many ways, had not thought of God and his creation in these terms, but rather as the divine Mind ordering pre-existent matter according to his Ideas like the Platonic Demiurge. The doctrines of God's transcendent infinity and of *creatio ex nihilo* are not spelt out in so many words in scripture any more than the doctrine of the Trinity is. The recognition of their coherence with one another, their importance for clarifying the apostolic tradition over against philosophical theory and Gnostic revelation alike, and their essential place in the framework which alone allows scripture to be interpreted appropriately, we owe largely to the work of Irenaeus. The framework of interpretation demanded the development of a systematic theology, related to the contents of scripture but not confined to them, deeply rooted in tradition yet not immobilised by it.

Modern scholars[1] have suggested that Irenaeus developed an essentially biblical theology, and that his thought was grounded in the perception of a 'salvation-history' which took account of 'stages' in God's plan of salvation. Both estimates are partly but not wholly right. Irenaeus was a man of his time, and as we have seen, his so-called biblical theology drew on much extra-biblical material, traditions like the fallen angel who became Satan as well as 'kerygmatic summaries' like the Rule of Faith, also philosophical arguments, or arguments from 'natural evidence' like the suggestion that it is natural for there to be four Gospels since there are four corners of the earth and four winds. In demonstrating the fulfilment of prophecies, Irenaeus did not eschew allegorical interpretation, despite his criticisms of Gnostic allegory: what was the difference? His allegory, he would argue, did not rearrange the pieces of mosaic, but was coherent with the unitive message of scripture as a whole as summarised in the Canon of Truth. Irenaeus' biblical theology could not claim to exist without traditions and canons of interpretation at once drawn from within the texts themselves and also external to them, belonging to a 'common semiotic system' embodied in the 'sociolinguistic community' of the Church.[2]

As for 'salvation-history', a careful look at his *Demonstration of the Apostolic Preaching*, rediscovered in 1904 in a manuscript in an Armenian monastery, soon shows that his perception was nothing like the 'evolutionary' view of God's revelation developed in modern theology. The work, which refers back to the treatise against heresies and is therefore later, is basically an exposition of the Christian faith written for one Marcianus. It takes the scriptures for granted, using them in ways traditional before his time: the bulk of scriptural quotation is from what we call the Old Testament, and von Campen-

1. e.g. J. Lawson, *The Biblical Theology of St Irenaeus*, London, 1948.
2. cf. Hans Frei, ' "Literal Reading" of Biblical Narrative in Christian Tradition' in *The Bible and the Narrative Tradition*, ed. Frank McConnell, OUP, 1986.

hausen suggests[1] that the changes in the perception of the Canon which Irenaeus himself began, have not affected his congregational preaching – here he seems not to have anything approaching a New Testament, which incidentally supports von Campenhausen's view that controversy made him innovative in terms of the Canon.

In other respects, however, we recognise the Irenaeus we have learned to know. One of the first things he does is produce yet another Rule of Faith, but one that incorporates not only the emphasis on creation, but also on recapitulation:

This then is the order of the rule of our faith, and the foundation of the building, and the stability of our conversation: God the Father, not made, not material, invisible; one God, the creator of all things: this is the first point of our faith. The second point is: The Word of God, Son of God, Christ Jesus our Lord, who was manifested to the prophets according to the form of their prophesying and according to the method of the dispensation of the Father: through whom all things were made; who also at the end of the times, to complete and gather up all things, was made man among men, visible and tangible, in order to abolish death and show forth life and produce a communion of union between God and man. And the third point is: The Holy Spirit, through whom the prophets prophesied, and the fathers learned the things of God, and the righteous were led forth into the way of righteousness; and who in the end of the times was poured out in a new way upon mankind in all the earth, renewing man unto God.

Next Irenaeus embarks on an exposition of this, showing how the baptism of regeneration rests on these three points, the Spirit leading to the Word, and the Word to the Father. The Father, Irenaeus insists, is God both of Jews and Gentiles, explaining that a covenant of adoption has been opened up in the end of the times. In explanation he appears to undertake a summary of the scriptural narrative, but it covers

1. *loc.cit.* p. 185.

only the Law-books (Genesis–Deuteronomy), and incorporates extra-biblical material, taking for granted, for example, the 'seven heavens' where powers and angels dwell. It is also selective: much space is expended on the creation of humanity, on Paradise and the Fall of Adam, on the stories confirming human disobedience, like Cain and Abel, Noah, the Tower of Babel, and on Abraham, the model of faith, with a rapid account of the descent into Egypt and the Exodus. Moses' legislation is not only intended to help the disobedient people to fear God and keep his commandments, but also contains prophecies of Christ, the calling of the Gentiles and the kingdom. After that, Irenaeus notes, a number of prophets were sent to herald the revelation of Christ to come.

At this point Irenaeus turns more or less directly from Law to Gospel, to the story of the incarnation, and the 'recapitulation' of Adam's mistake in Christ. But there is no interest shown in the narratives or teachings of the Gospel books themselves: birth, death and resurrection alone really matter. The rest of the book shows how the promises to Abraham and David were fulfilled in Christ, how the restoration of humanity was prophesied in the scriptures, and so their fulfilment confirms the truth of God. This is a brilliant exposition of the traditional proof from prophecy, highly selective in its use of scripture, neither a narrative, nor a theology with any real sense of the biblical story presenting a 'salvation-history'; the accommodation of the old scriptures was not by an idea of 'progressive revelation' through God's involvement in history, but by typology, a technique to which we will devote more attention in the next chapter.

The point is surely made: proper performance of scripture for Irenaeus depends in the end not on canons of interpretation offered by the scriptures themselves, nor on a sense of context within the flow of an overarching narrative history, but rather on 'the plan of salvation', on what we might call the Christian kerygma, on a framework belonging to the particular community which designates these books as authoritative, a framework related to these books but 'extra' to them, a framework passed down openly in a tradition guaranteed as ancient and reliable, but honed and refined by theological argument, modified by controversy, thought through in a systematic way to meet the needs of the times. The extent to which this 'novelty' was apparent to Irenaeus himself may be questionable; yet his creative performance of the repertoire involved selection, development and clarification, unconscious though it may have been.

Meanwhile the canon has long been effectively closed. Does this put us in a markedly different situation from Irenaeus? Does it undermine our analogy with the classic repertoire, allowing us to envisage a fixed relationship between the components of the canon such as is unknown in other contexts? Does the traditional order of the books properly affect the way they are read? Could there be an intratextual key after all, a 'canonical' interpretation which obviates the need for an extratextual framework? I fear experience since the Reformation tells against such a view being convincing.

The integration of scripture within tradition, so natural to Irenaeus, was torn asunder by the Reformation. The performance of a classic sometimes necessitates challenge to the accretion of tradition, and that is what happened. The unfortunate result has been that the tradition, by becoming controversial, has acquired a separate existence alongside scripture in Catholic as well as Protestant argumentation, while the Bible has had to bear authority independent of the tradition which once provided the canons of classic interpretation. The watchword *sola scriptura* has proved a very mixed blessing, eventually spawning not only fundamentalism but a protestantism which has proved inherently fissiparous as different groups have interpreted the texts differently, unaware of the fact that frameworks external to the text are inevitable, that each would be bound to develop its own tradition, its own canons of interpretation, its own framework, which owes something but not everything to scripture itself. In practice it has been found that the various strands of scripture cannot be given equal weight, and the Lutheran search for the appropriate 'canon within the canon' is indicative that scripture does not offer its own key to its interpretation. This should give pause to any who are tempted to espouse literary theories about intratextual interpretation, or hastily imagine the key lies in the fact of canonicity.

In fact a number of Christian scholars have asked in recent decades whether the Bible has not been asked to bear too much weight, whether the appropriate place of scripture in Christianity may not be quite different from its place is Islam, and indeed Judaism. Is it not significant that the Koran is never translated, and Hebrew is the language of synagogue reading, whereas Christianity has had no such attachment to the original texts, but has made its sacred writings available in most of the languages under the sun? What is central to Christianity is not a text, it is said, but a person, namely Christ. The books of Holy Scripture were problematic from the beginning, for the only way the Jewish scriptures could be appropriated was by abandoning the 'letter' for the 'spirit', re-reading them in a Christological way, and then subordinating them to the New Testament. Even then the books were testimony to something other than themselves, rather than a sacred text. Biblicism, then, is not only fissiparous, but fundamentally false to the true character of Christianity. The great mistake was the closing of the canon, the painting of a defining halo around documents which should never have been so sacralised, a mistake compounded by the Reformation controversies.[1]

Undoubtedly there is a considerable element of truth in this, but the problems would be eased if we could take seriously the important balance between scripture, tradition and theological thinking implied by the work of Irenaeus, for whom of course the canon was not yet firmly closed, yet to whom scripture appeared both sacred and central. Now that almost the only thing held in common by all those who call themselves Christian is this canon of sacred books, the Bible is quite simply indispensable. But faced with the fragmentation of the sociolinguistic community to which the Canon and the canons of interpretation belong, self-consciousness

1. John Barton, *People of the Book?* SPCK, 1988, is the most recent treatment of the issues.

needs to be fostered about the various interpretative frameworks brought to the text, inherited as they are from differing
group traditions within Christianity, and based partly on
abstraction of intratextual elements, partly on extratextual
theological assumptions. Then the Canon of scripture which
we hold in common, and the frameworks we do not, can be
integrated through tough theological thinking and dialogue
of a creative kind.

For classic performance of the repertoire must avoid sec-
tarian interpretation, and this requires, on the one hand, an
awareness of the whole repertoire and the place of each part
in the whole, a kind of 'canon criticism' in the sense of
knowing the overall canonical context, and on the other an
understanding of the common classic tradition of performance, roughly speaking the framework enshrined in the creeds.
But inspired performance cannot be limited by the text or
tied to tradition – it must allow for creative play, for challenge
to the tradition in the light of scholarly investigation, or
development of it under the impetus of new cultural contexts.
Irenaeus may be said to have produced the first systematic
theology, a theology deeply embedded in tradition and scripture, but forced to develop, to impose coherence on its inheritance, as the only way of preserving an essentially biblical and
traditional stance in new circumstances. We could do worse
than follow in his footsteps.

But we are faced not only with the fragmentation of the
sociolinguistic community to which the Christian Bible and
the canons of interpretation belong, but also with a post-
Christian and pluralistic culture in which agnostics, atheists
and people of other faiths have access to this literature. Indeed
with our changed perspectives, we would do well to feel
embarrassed about the way our forebears, in such a high-
handed and insensitive way, commandeered the sacred books
that really belong to the on-going Jewish community. Do not
these others have a right to read these books and interpret
them without the tyranny of 'frameworks' which insist,
though with hardly an altogether united voice, upon the
essential unity of these texts and their coherence with the
Christian 'system'? Do we not have to admit that the Bible

as literature belongs to the wider canon of 'world literature', that in a sense it is a classic that belongs to all? Surely we do, and once more we are confronted by the need to do justice to a kind of 'dual character'.

As human literature the Bible belongs to human culture, and may be read by any reader. Different readers bring different 'horizons' to the text – indeed some would argue that the reader 'creates' the text, and the text in itself has no meaning until it is 'received' by the reader's imagination filling in the interstices and investing the text with meaning.[1] Certainly a 'non-Christian' reader will not bring the same framework to the reading of the texts, and can claim to read them from fresh perspectives for that very reason. Anti-canonical readings are inevitable.

Nevertheless, for all readers, whatever their beliefs or frameworks, such literature is illuminated by a knowledge of the place of the particular text in the 'classic repertoire', by its earthing in its original cultural context, whether historical, geographical, political or social, by the recognition of its various genres, of differing styles and dates, and all the particularities which enable us to enter imaginatively the world of the text. It is possible to enter that world without making connections with the real world, though literature would cease to be significant if it became no more than escapist fantasy, and generally classics survive because they are recognised to have some 'universal' validity, some inherent 'authority' or inspirational character.

So to read any text fruitfully requires entering it as a 'possibly true' world, and it is a fact of experience that people with or without dogmatic commitment can read the biblical literature as they would read Shakespeare or Greek tragedy

---

1. Some of the 'classic' discussions of 'deconstruction' and 'reader-reception theory' can be found in *Modern Criticism and Theory: A Reader*, ed. David Lodge, Longman, 1988. The criticisms of M. H. Abrams and E. D. Hirsch reinforce the position adopted in this book. The notion of 'horizons' and the hermeneutics of Gadamer will be more familiar to readers acquainted with hermeneutical theory in theology: see H. G. Gadamer, *Truth and Method*, New York, Seabury, 1975; A. Thiselton, *The Two Horizons*, Paternoster, 1981; W. Jeanrond, *cit.sup.*

or the Bhagavad Gita, and gain insights, or a sense of disclosure, or find deep chords of recognition and response touched through that experience. Such reading may be enhanced by scholarship, or illuminated by the latest movements in literary criticism, just as in the case of any other literary text. It may be deepened by careful attention to the precise details of the text, an aspect of performance to which we will turn in Chapter 5. But the immediate point is that such reading need not depend on any supposed overall unity of the 'canon', whether understood on the broad scale, or on the narrower scale of reference to the books conventionally grouped as the Bible. There would appear to be no need in this wider context for a 'framework' of interpretation such as Irenaeus found necessary. It is to this common literary world that Biblical Studies belong, and they hold their rightful place alongside parallel studies in the Humanities. Here the closure of the canon seems not significant, and canonical interpretation positively obscurantist.

In the present situation, to recognise the Bible as both universal in this sense, as well as particular to its 'proper' sociolinguistic community, is the only way to do it justice. This 'dual character' should not be regarded as simplistically coterminous with the 'Two Natures' view which would attribute both divine and human properties to this text. For the general reader may consciously or unconsciously touch the transcendent and universal here, as in any other classic text; and the reader of the Word of God is reading human words. Yet one context keeps us mindful of the Bible's 'humanity' and its continuity with all literature; the other context requires that it should also be read as Holy Scripture. Those of us who are committed to the Bible have to learn to read it competently in both ways.

4

Jewish Texts and Christian Meanings

The individual works within a repertoire are never entirely unrelated. It is not just that they all belong to a developing tradition of composition, or that composers are inevitably influenced by their predecessors, whether creatively imitating or deliberately reacting against them, but that works which aim to become classic frequently refer to earlier classic works by quotation or allusion. Within a particular work the role of repetition, recurring themes, development and recapitulation, and conversely internal opposites, contrasting themes, tempos, moods, keys, and so on, is even more important. The dynamics of music, or any other art form, depend on disjunctive as well as unitive features, on dissonance as well its resolution in harmony. This is particularly true in relation to a given individual composition, but important also when works are chosen to be performed alongside one another in a concert programme, and not inapplicable to the relationship between works within a wider corpus.

Now these features may be flattened out by a performance which attends too much to the general overarching perspective, or they may be highlighted so as to contribute to a sense of direction and progress. Recurring or contrasting themes may provide shape leading up to appropriate culmination in an ending, a coda or cadence that rounds off the whole. So can it be said that there is a kind of 'ground' in the Bible on which variations are played? Or is it rather that there are complex interrelating and contrasting themes, to which full justice must be done for a masterly performance to be possible? What is the role of quotation and allusion – is it mere repetition or creative renewal? What about the sense of an

66

ending, of preparation for a finale? Do interpretative frameworks necessarily flatten out the important shades and contrasts? Is the 'secular' reading of the Bible a necessary corrective to its 'sacred' reading, lest the individuality of its
components be suppressed?

Irenaeus, as we have seen, exploited the idea of 'recapitulation', and it was a recapitulation beyond mere repetition in
that the replay 'reversed' the original theme as it ran over
the ground again. There was both contrast and fulfilment as
type and antitype were brought into relation with one
another. For Irenaeus this creative recapitulation of the
'theme' provided the direction of the 'piece', giving it its unity
and focus, from the past, into the present and the future, and
so to the End when the purposes of God would be brought
to their full fruition. His Rule of Faith framework enabled
him to discern a shape running through the score itself, and
then to relate to that a whole range of subsidiary 'themes' as
he noted one 'fulfilment' after another, one 'type' after
another, in the replay or quotation of texts. In a sense this
merely picked up the long-standing early Christian 'proof
from prophecy', but in another sense it pioneered the development of a full-blown Christological interpretation of the old
scriptures, both ensuring their subservience to the new, and
disastrously flattening future performance of both old and
new texts. Typology and allegory each played their part.

But this 'flattening' process was not entirely inevitable,
and is not really characteristic of Irenaeus himself or his
predecessors. If we go back to earlier Christian thinkers like
Paul and the author of Hebrews, we can discern a remarkable
two-way process going on in which the texts of the old scriptures still stood in their own right but were brought into
dialogue with current attempts to understand the meaning
and implication of recent events. If Christ in some sense
provided the key to the true meaning of the old scriptures, so
that "when a man turns to the Lord, the veil (over people's
minds when they read Moses) is removed" (2 Cor. 3:16),
what is even clearer is the reverse, the fact that the old
scriptures provided the insights, the themes and patterns,

that enabled people to make sense of Jesus Christ, and indeed of their own lives and experience as the vitality of 'new life' was poured out among them. It seemed like the beginning of the End to which the prophecies had pointed, and suddenly the texts themselves sprang into life in a way that they had not before. New discoveries were made as the scriptures were searched, as new insights highlighted things that were there all the time but given little emphasis in previous performance: suddenly their significance was noted by hindsight, as it were. None of this had the effect of 'flattening' performance, but rather produced a creatively new reading.[1]

A whole set of basic assumptions about God and his dealings with his chosen people could simply be taken for granted as the backcloth to this new deal in Christ, simply because the scriptures were given, so their 'themes', their images, their prescriptions, their stories, their characters could be alluded to, could provide models, could be creatively quoted and re-performed. This was particularly true of passages which seemed to throw light on the offence of the cross, and to permit understanding of it as part of God's will and plan for salvation. The structures for dealing with sin provided by God under the Law were the required presuppositions for grasping the sacrificial significance of the death of Christ: this might be treated as fulfilling and abrogating the old mechanisms at a practical level, yet the texts with their categories of thought remained determinative of understanding. Without the Day of Atonement, atonement in Christ would be without context; without the Passover and Exodus, liberation in Christ would be scarcely discerned.

At this stage, then, we find the seeds of Christological interpretation, but to a considerable extent the flow of traffic is reversed: Christ was illuminated by the scriptures, rather than the scriptures subordinated to him. There was a genuine sense of recapitulation which allowed the significance of the original to stand alongside its replay, even to be rediscovered

1. The study of the New Testament's use of scripture has produced an enormous bibliography. For further discussion of some of the points in this paragraph, the reader is referred to Frances Young and David F. Ford, *Meaning and Truth in 2 Corinthians*, SPCK, 1987, ch. 3.

behind the accretion of tradition. This remains the case in much Second-Century typology, though the interplay of type and antitype runs back and forth in a way that sometimes appears to anticipate the later thorough-going interpretation of the old scriptures as prophetic of Christ and virtually nothing else.

An examination of an example which has itself become a kind of classic will help to illustrate the point. It was in 1936 that C. Bonner identified the unknown homily found four years before in a Fifth-Century papyrus codex as the work of Melito, well-known bishop of Sardis in the Second Century.[1] The rediscovered text was clearly the work known to the ancient church as *Concerning the Pascha*, the word *pascha* ambiguously referring both to the Passover, which transliterated into Greek as Pascha, and by false Greek etymology to the Passion. It is probably significant that Melito belonged to a group of Christians in Asia Minor who celebrated the Passion of Christ in close association with the Jewish Passover, namely on 14th Nisan, the Day of Preparation, on which according to John's Gospel Jesus died at the moment when the Passover lambs were being killed in the Temple. These Quartodecimans, as they were known from the Latin for fourteen, came into conflict with the bishop of Rome: for Roman practice was far less closely tied to the Jewish calendar, fixing their 'passion-day' on a Friday so that the Day of Resurrection fell three days later on the first day of the week.

For Melito, then, Passover and Passion were naturally associated because of the calendar. Yet this homily gives no clues at all about how the Quartodecimans celebrated their festival, nor does it reflect any Jewish Passover practices. The whole depends on scriptural texts, presenting us with an elaborate typological parallel between the Exodus-story and the Passion-narrative. Clearly Christians did not reinterpret Jewish traditional practice in the light of Christ: rather they went back behind tradition to the scriptures, re-read them and produced a new performance. Reports in the works of

1. Text and translation in *Melito of Sardis: On Pascha and Fragments*, ed. Stuart George Hall, Oxford Early Christian Texts, 1979.

Josephus suggest that Jews of his day thought that the events of the Exodus would be replayed at the time of the Messiah, and hints in the New Testament suggest that such ideas were operative in the earliest Christian communities: according to John 6, Jesus the Messiah brought manna in the wilderness, bread from heaven. Here we find an elaborate and detailed working out of that fundamental perspective:

> The scripture from the Hebrew Exodus has been read
> and the words of the mystery have been plainly stated,
>> how the sheep is sacrificed
>> and how the people is saved
>> and how Pharaoh is scourged through the mystery.
> Understand, therefore, beloved,
> how it is new and old,
>> eternal and temporary,
>> perishable and imperishable,
>> mortal and immortal, this mystery of the Pascha . . .
>
> For instead of the lamb there was a Son,
>> and instead of the sheep a Man,
>> and in the Man Christ who comprised all things.

With such a prologue, Melito goes on to rehearse the Exodus story in his own rhetorical manner, assimilating the narrative to the high-flown drama of Greek tragedy, graphically bringing out the horror of the death of the first-born with imaginative flourishes. Then he sums up the story:

Such was the calamity that encompassed Egypt,
  and suddenly made her childless.
But Israel was guarded by the slaughter of the sheep,
  and was even illuminated together by the shed blood,
and the death of the sheep became a wall for the people.
O strange and inexpressible mystery!
The slaughter of the sheep was found to be Israel's salvation,
and the death of the sheep became the people's life,
  and the blood won the angel's respect.

So far the story has had its autonomy. But now Melito

suggests that the fulfilment or antitype has retrospective power:

Tell me, angel, what did you respect?
  The slaughter of the sheep or the life of the Lord?
  The death of the sheep or the type of the Lord?
  The blood of the sheep or the spirit of the Lord?
It is clear that your respect was won
when you saw the mystery of the Lord occurring in the sheep,
  the life of the Lord in the slaughter of the lamb,
  the type of the Lord in the death of the sheep;
that is why you did not strike Israel,
  but made only Egypt childless.

What is interesting here is that the original story still stands, the type providing an explanation, integrating with it rather than replacing it: its power as model or type requires that it stand up alongside what it prefigures, gaining significance from it. So it is not reduced to a mere Christological cypher. Now, however, Melito spells out what he means by a 'type'. He draws an analogy with an architect's model, an artist's sketch, a sculptor's figurine:

  . . . a preliminary sketch is made of the future thing
    out of wax or of clay or of wood,
  in order that what will soon arise
    taller in height,
    and stronger in power,
    and beautiful in form,
    and rich in its construction,
  may be seen through a small and perishable sketch.

Of course the emphasis on the 'perishability' of the sketch begins the tipping of the balance. For

  . . . to each belongs a proper season:
    a proper time for the model,
    a proper time for the material,
    a proper time for the reality.

71

You make the model;
   you want that
    because you see in it the image of the future thing.
You produce the material before the model;
   you want that
    because of what is going to arise in it.
You complete the work;
   you want that alone,
   you love that alone,
because in it alone you see the pattern and the material and
   the reality.

As for the Epistle to the Hebrews the new covenant being 'better' renders the old obsolescent. Yet the balance has not tipped so far that the recapitulation makes the first statement otiose, flattening out the texture of the drama. Melito proceeds to tell a new story, a story of another slave cast in prison and in need of rescue, of his descendants trapped by the powers of sin and death, of man made in God's image, enclosed by a "strange disaster and captivity", "dragged off a prisoner under the shadows of death". He tells how the Lord made prior arrangements in patriarchs and prophets, prefiguring the mystery to come:

  Therefore if you wish to see the mystery of the Lord,
  look at Abel who is similarly murdered,
    at Isaac who is similarly bound,
    at Joseph who is similarly sold,
    at Moses who is similarly exposed,
    at David who is similarly persecuted,
  at the prophets who similarly suffer for the sake of Christ.
  Look also at the sheep which is slain in the land of Egypt,
    which struck Egypt
    and saved Israel by its blood.

Melito sees that discernment of the mystery of Christ depends upon looking at the types, not vice versa, and so this noting of parallels and repetitions, followed by quotation of key prophetic utterances, highlights their importance. The telling of the passion-story then exploits allusions, keeping the dynamic relationship between type and antitype:

> For, himself led as a lamb,
>   and slain as a sheep,
>   he ransomed us from the world's service
>   as from the land of Egypt,
>   and freed us from the devil's slavery
>   as from the hand of Pharaoh;
>   and he marked our souls with his own Spirit
>   and the members of our body with his own blood . . .

> It is he that delivered us from slavery to liberty,
>   from darkness to light,
>   from death to life,
>   from tyranny to eternal royalty,
> and made us a new priesthood
>   and an eternal people personal to him.
> He is the Pascha of our salvation . . .

> It is he that was enfleshed in a virgin,
>   that was hanged on a tree,
>   that was buried in the earth,
>   that was raised from the dead,
>   that was taken up to the heights of heaven.
> He is the lamb being slain . . .

So as we have seen, there are signs of the shift towards a Christological interpretation which empties the old scriptures of meaning, but the relationship is still complex. In other ways we have to handle complexity in this text. If Rome thought Melito and his fellow-Quartodecimans too Jewish, the next part of the homily is the first really bitter Christian attack on the Jews as the ones responsible for the death of Christ. It does not make nice reading. It reminds us that what one is closest to, if there be a breakdown of relationships, is precisely what one is most hostile to. Of course we should not overlook the fact that at this stage the Christians were a small, marginalised group, vulnerable because they were neither proper Jews nor proper Gentiles, and faced in Sardis by a prosperous and sizeable Jewish community, whose very presence was a constant threat to Christian claims. The early Christian communities had identity problems, and were dogged by 'judaising' tendencies. So sadly the seeds of a shameful future were sown here: he had to die, Melito admits – it was part of God's plan – but it need not have been *you*, God's own people acting against their own Lord.

The important point to notice is this complexity of relationship: the Jewish scriptures are fundamental, and for Melito there are no others. The significance of the Passover is seen by going back behind traditional practice and re-reading the story in the text from a new perspective. The very perspective from which the story is re-read was anticipated in Jewish expectation, and now by hindsight the scriptures gain new power, not least because the highlighting of 'repetitions' and 'quotations' and 'recapitulations' provides the necessary clues to the meaning of the mystery of Christ. They make it possible to trace the shape of God's overall plan of salvation and enable a sense of direction towards an ending. Yet for all that there is sharp contrast, there is darkness and difference, obsolescence, abolition; law is opposed to Gospel, type to reality:

Once the slaying of the sheep was precious,
   but it is worthless now because of the life of the Lord;
the death of the sheep was precious,
   but it is worthless now because of the salvation of the Lord;
the blood of the sheep was precious,
   but it is worthless now because of the Spirit of the Lord;
a speechless lamb was precious,
   but it is worthless now because of the spotless Son;
the temple below was precious,
   but it is worthless now because of the Christ above.

Some modern scholarship[1] has seen the power of this kind of typology, and has attempted to 'rescue' it from the rejection consequent upon the development of the historico-critical

1. Especially Lampe and Woollcombe, *Essays in Typology*, SCM, 1957.

method. This attempt depends on the possibility of distinguishing it from 'allegory' and from the rather wooden 'proof-text' approach to the fulfilment of prophecy. For alongside 'typology' we find these other techniques even within the New Testament itself: Matthew takes a delight in pointing out that certain things happened the way they did in order to fulfil a prophecy, which is then quoted; Hebrews makes Christ an eternal priest after the order of Melchisedek by using typical allegorical techniques.

Of course everyone admits that such hermeneutical tricks were part of the culture to which the early church belonged. The ancient world even conducted war and affairs of state by consulting oracles and auspices, and by the time of the Roman Empire, there were collections of Sibylline Oracles in books available for the purpose.[1] Jews and later Christians latched on to this, producing their own books of Sibylline Oracles showing how the pagan prophets confirmed the truth of the Jewish ones.[2] It is not surprising that under these sorts of pressures the Jewish scriptures were assumed to be books of prophetic prediction, and even before Christians adopted this method of interpretation, the Messianic hopes of many Jewish circles had provoked the construction of ideal scenarios on the basis of the words of the scriptural prophecies. This procedure required 'unpacking the riddles' by allegory; for in Greek literature it was taken for granted the Delphic Oracle spoke in an obscure way, and that seeing through the riddle was essential. Matthew's piecemeal procedure is anticipated by the Dead Sea Scrolls, in each case a sentence or saying being treated as an independent 'oracle' predicting a particular happening. This is not to say that there was no precedent in the biblical material. The classic contrast between 'foretelling' and 'forthtelling' does not do justice to the element of 'consultation' and 'prediction' in the pre-exilic Israelite prophetic movement: witness, for example, the story of Micaiah-ben-

1. See H. W. Parke, *Sibyls and Sibylline Prophecy in Classical Antiquity*, ed. B. C. McGing, Routledge, 1988.
2. These can be found in translation with introduction and notes in *The Old Testament Pseudepigrapha*, Vol. I, *Apocalyptic Literature and Testaments*, ed. James H. Charlesworth, DLT, 1983.

Imla (1 Kgs 22). Such parallels made this set of common assumptions about the genre of ancient sacred books entirely natural.

Alongside this, allegorical interpretation of literature was commonplace. It is hard for us to appreciate how the ancients felt about literature: all ancient texts had a kind of sacred aura, and Homer was read not just for its literary values, but for its moral influence.[1] The great poets were committed to memory, and speech and writing larded with apposite quotations. There was a mystery about words committed to writing so that they could last beyond their authors and seem 'eternal', and poets were inspired by divine beings like the Muses. The antiquity of texts added to their authority. Here was wisdom. But such an attitude necessarily induced a tendency to 'apply' the words of literature to contemporary life. To find morals meant some degree of allegory, to find philosophical truth meant reading the whole as a cypher for something else. Jewish treatment of the Bible was not identical, yet some of the same instincts were operative, and the deducing of Halakah from the texts of Torah involved its own kind of allegory. Apocalyptic, with its highly symbolic method and style, depended on allegory: the meaning was meant to be hidden and accessible only to those in the know.

The Christological reading of the Jewish scriptures had its grounding in such assumptions: that ancient literature was sacred, oracular, and allegorical. Texts were to be pondered until their present application became clear. They were mysterious, and meant to be. The true meaning lay not in the literal or historical reference, but rather in the 'fulfilment', the reality to which the text pointed.

The historico-critical movement has consistently refused to accept that such is an appropriate way to treat texts. So Isaiah 7:14, "Behold a virgin shall conceive", is a mistranslation to start with, and certainly was intended to have an immediate reference in Isaiah's word to Ahaz, rather than being a Messianic prediction: what the reference originally was became

---

1. Edwin Hatch, *The Influence of Greek Ideas on Christianity*, Hibbert Lectures 1888, brilliantly expounds this point.

the preoccupation of researchers (and speculators!). To arrive at the 'plain sense' of scripture meant reconstructing the historical context, and stripping away the accretion of allegorical nonsense. If the Christological meaning of the Old Testament disappeared in the process, so much the worse for Christian tradition.

The rejection of the notion of prophecy in this sense has been one of the areas where fundamentalists have felt strongly that so-called 'liberals' have sold out, and it is true that one of its consequences has been the tendency of 'liberal' Christians to pay scant regard to the Old Testament. But the other reaction has been to create a new framework for accommodating it. History and evolution being the cultural air in which the historico-critical method blossomed, the notion of 'progressive revelation' came into vogue, as we saw in the first chapter. Much in the Old Testament was 'primitive', and many of the ideas of God had to be corrected in the light of the revelation of Christ. Nevertheless, it was in Israelite religion that the prophetic movement germinated the idea of 'ethical monotheism', perceiving both the oneness of God and his moral character. So the seeds of a 'higher religion' were planted, and the way prepared for Christ. Greek philosophy may have reached the same conclusions, but it was never embodied in a 'living faith' in the same way. The full revelation of God came in the New Testament, but it was the culmination of progressive realisation of the truth in Israelite history.

Now this approach was really rather optimistic, failing to do proper justice to the unevenness of the process. It also presupposed a linear development of a single theme towards its denouement, and it did not allow for repetition, allusion, quotation, recapitulation, never mind contrast or opposition. So the defenders of typology[1] suggested that typological parallels were not excluded by such historical consciousness after all. Seeing events as recapitulations bore witness to the consistency of the patterns of God's dealings with humanity, to the workings of providence in history. So while the notion of

1. e.g. Lampe and Woollcombe, *cit.sup.*

predictive oracles and the use of allegory was still to be spurned, typology could be reclaimed.

The difficulty with this approach is that the distinction its promulgators wanted to make is not in practice clear. Most examples of typology involve some measure of allegory, for reading one story in terms of another necessitates turning elements of the story into symbol: so the virgin Eve may seem neatly parallel to the virgin Mary, but the cross is not really a tree in a sense directly and obviously parallel to the tree of knowledge. Effective poetic association it may be, suitable for devotion and imaginative contemplation, but it is nevertheless a form of allegory. But the defenders of typology might not wish to press that example since history matters so much to them, and they probably find the historical character of the Adam and Eve story somewhat problematical. So what about Melito's typology between the Exodus and salvation in Christ? It would seem a classic example of exactly what these scholars want: God bringing salvation in parallel events. But if Melito himself does not immediately appear to resort to allegory (though inevitably he cannot really avoid it), his successors certainly did: the bitter herbs, the fact that the Israelites carried no stave, and all the little details of the Exodus were given spiritual meanings in subsequent Paschal Homilies, and the slippage from what might be regarded as 'pure typology' to 'muddy allegory' is far from precise. In any case radical critics have even questioned the historicity of the Exodus!

The problem arises from the imposition on ancient texts of a framework arising from modern preoccupation with history. Of course ancient culture produced history writing and ancient people revered antiquity. But the obsession with factuality, with tracing cause and effect, with development, means that for a modern theologian to affirm that Christianity is a historical religion carries all kinds of implications unsuspected by either the biblical writers or their earliest interpreters.[1] Irenaeus, as we have seen, did not really have

1. James Barr, *Explorations in Theology 7*, SCM, 1980, pp. 31ff, suggests that at least six different things are meant by 'Christianity is a historical religion' in modern theology.

a sense of 'salvation-history' or 'biblical theology' akin to modern ideas, despite such ideas being so frequently attributed to him. For him the important point about Christ was not that he was 'historical' but that he was REAL. The danger was that people so disparaged the material world they found it offensive to drag Christ down to it, and so were lured into docetic Christologies, then into unreal liturgies in which the bread and wine were merely symbolic of spiritual reality and not eucharist for the good things of creation.

We have seen that Irenaeus could produce a conspectus of the Pentateuchal story, and he had a sense of humanity's ancient disobedience being reversed in Christ which enabled him to make sense both of the stories of the beginning of things, and the narratives of God's dealings with Israel. But many of the events of Israel's history held little interest for him, for history was not his real concern. His overview was highly selective because significance did not lie simply in the happenedness or development of things. He did have a sense of sequence, and an expectation that as there had been a beginning so there would be an end. But within that 'linear' scheme he was prepared to see anticipations, repetitions, recapitulations, reversals, ups and downs. In this he was more realistic than modern scholars who have imagined a sharp contrast between the biblical sense of time in terms of a linear-eschatological model and so-called cyclical views supposedly current in the Hellenistic world. Cycles may belong to Stoic philosophy, and the idea of the End of the world to apocalyptic, but Greek historians were fascinated by the interplay of divine and human purpose, by fate and destiny, in the outworking of heroic characters and events, and much of the Bible is no more linear-eschatological than that.

The fact of the matter is that the Bible is composite, a library of different genres, neither straightforwardly a narrative nor a history in our sense. Scholars have realised this, of course, and by critical processes have tried to reconstruct the history behind the texts. They have then made those events bear the weight of revelation rather than the biblical text. But this obscures the complexity of 'history'. Of course there is a sense in which facts can be traced, and fact and interpretation distinguished – detectives depend on the possibility of such analysis and reconstruction. But 'history' is not just 'fact': it is a corporate memory conveying identity, telling where we have come from so that we can know who we are and where we are going.

All such story-telling depends on selection and highlighting, picking out what is significant, focusing on values and directions, forgetting the daily nitty-gritty in the interests of perspective. Ancient historians knew that their purpose was 'moral', that history was a 'possession for ever', that it was literature exploring the same features of human life as tragic drama, its nobility and transience, the effects of sin or the sense of fate, the ambiguities of war or of conflicting loyalties, hopes, fears, loves, hates, ambition, empire, tyranny, the pride that comes before a fall. In this they were but slightly more sophisticated than the tribal bard. In a sense there is no 'history' but what people make of it. The Bible bears witness to the community memory of the Israelites and the Church, rather than to supposedly discrete 'events' of revelation or salvation-history. It is part of 'tradition'. It presupposes history only in the sense that 'literature' in oral or written form shapes that memory into a sense of a meaningful past.

Now if we stop making the 'event' bear the weight of revelation, and see how significance is 'placed' on events, then the process of making allusions and quotations, of telling one story in terms of another, or against another, becomes entirely natural. For centuries simple Christian believers have 'read themselves' in the Bible, and shaped the telling of their personal stories by such parallels: so "I had my Damascus Road at a set of traffic lights in Dudley!" Christian nations or races have done the same thing: the Exodus modelling the Great Trek of the Afrikaners, or the black slaves' escape route from the southern States to the North. It is not the history that matters so much as the 'type', the possibility of a recapitulation that makes sense of experience. The expectation should be that a theme has many variations, some contrasting in tone and tempo, some elaborating, some simplifying. Recent biblical criticism has focused on the constant process of interpretation and reinterpretation that has formed the texts into the rich deposit we now have: is it surprising that the process went on?

The notions of 'progressive revelation', or of 'salvation-history', or of a 'biblical theology' with concepts unique to historical Israel, were modern ideas or 'frameworks' imposed on the Bible, eventually to be undermined by the techniques of historico-criticism which produced them: for it can be shown they are not inherent in the Bible.[1] Typology, on the other hand, allows us to see how many texts and narratives within the Bible actually work, and how they may continue to work, through allusion, quotation, repetition, development, recapitulation. The trouble with that, however, is the lack of any criteria for determining what may or may not be read into the text by hindsight, and we may also feel disturbed by the inherent tendency for typology to shade over into allegory and make crude predictions seem plausible.

But the other problem with these modern frameworks lies with their sense of ending. For they either 'stop' with Jesus Christ, who becomes the coda to which the linear theme was leading up all along, or they appear to espouse an on-going progressive history with no obvious culmination. And while typology often seems eschatological by its very nature, the kind of open-ended typology that has been suggested leaves us with the same unresolved dilemma: is Jesus Christ the finale, or is it rather the End of the world?

A sense of ending is vital for understanding the work being performed, whether it be music, drama or opera. The climax, be it expected or unexpected, provides the perspective which makes sense of the whole, and until it is reached there can be nothing but uncertainty or expectation or suspense. Clearly the individual pieces in the biblical repertoire have each their own ending, some more clearly than others – critics often discuss the odd ending of Mark, or what meaning is intended by the curiously undramatic ending with which Acts is provided. But can it be said that the Bible has an overall ending? Is there a coda or finale that retrospectively 'explains' the

1. James Barr, *loc.cit.*

theme or themes, the variations, the recapitulations, the contrasts, the *da capo*, the modulations of key? There is perhaps a serious question whether a work can be performed at all if there is no definite ending, and so in this case, whether the closure of the canon is deceptive and the Bible can only be treated as a fairly arbitrary collection of pieces to be independently performed.

One answer might be that the Book of Revelation provides an ending, not by narrating it but by projecting it, through vision and prophecy indicating what the ending will be. The ending of the Bible is the End of the world, and so its text encompasses everything, from alpha to omega, from the beginning to the end of all things. Thus the proper performance of the Bible necessitates an eschatology, an orientation towards the future, and theories of progressive revelation or of religious evolution with no climax ultimately fail. It is not for nothing that fundamentalist groups are fascinated by Revelation, and sense in the possibility of nuclear holocaust the arrival of the 'apocalyptic' cataclysm. So far from 'progressing', human history brings wars and rumours of wars, and the horrors that precede the End are evident. The only problem for that kind of view is that for Revelation Omega is God, not a man-made nuclear weapon.

Another answer finds the end in Christ: for he fulfilled all the prophecies. So the true religion is revealed in Christianity, all other revelations are partial, Christ is final. That is somewhat crudely stated, but it was to such a conclusion that the Christological interpretation of the Old Testament naturally led, and this kind of thinking underlies the triumphalism of Christianity down the ages, both political and intellectual and spiritual. It has particularly fuelled Christian scorn of Jews who still await their Messiah. And these days it fuels the kind of Christianity which speaks of Jesus being Lord of all the earth, of his power bringing healing and renewal, sinlessness and perfection to those born again or baptised in the Spirit. It may sometimes be more subtly expressed in terms of the uniqueness of Jesus, but however put, it draws the ending firmly into the past: all is already accomplished and the Kingdom of God is here. The story is over. The only problem with that is that it is clearly refuted by ordinary experience: Christ is not obviously King nor Lord of all the earth – many do not know him or accept him; sorrow and sighing, sin, sickness and suffering, death and evil are still characteristic of our lives and our experience; there is no peace and justice on the earth; the End is clearly not yet, the Kingdom was not 'spread' through the missionary movement and is unlikely to be brought in by the next revolution.

One thing biblical criticism has teased out is the fact that this tension between 'now' and 'not yet' was there in Christianity from the beginning. The 'end' was in a sense Christ, the fulfilment of all that had gone before, the recapitulation of human destiny, the fruition of God's purposes for humankind. It was that sense which was articulated in the rather wooden application of predictive texts, in the imaginative associations of typology, in what seems to us the twisted reasoning of allegory. Yet clearly the Kingdom had not visibly arrived, and the powers of evil still stalked the earth. The prophecies of power and glory still had to come to pass. Meanwhile the resurrection was the 'beginning of the end', and the gift of the Spirit was a 'downpayment' on the future, and the eucharist was a foretaste of the feast of the Kingdom. The End-process was initiated, so that the wrath and judgment of God on all the 'gonewrongness' of the present order was revealed as well as his grace and his righteousness in saving the elect. The whole creation was groaning with birthpangs, as the new heaven and earth were coming into being. Little wonder they expected the End immediately. But also little wonder that disappointment about the date did not destroy the faith. For Christ was the 'key' to the ultimate which made possible continued living in the penultimate.

In time the Kingdom was projected on to the heavens, and salvation became life after death. But in the process the way was left open for a splitting apart of the creative tension between 'ending' and 'no ending'. Failure to live with the tension lies at the root of all triumphalism, and all preoccupation with End of the world prophecy, for all these are ways of 'flattening' things out by choosing one out of two possible endings and subordinating everything else in the text to it.

Paradoxically the ending requires open-endedness. Christ 'anticipates' the ending, provides some key to the whole, gives enough clue for our penultimate lives to be drawn into the patterns of theme and variation and recapitulation, but the end is not yet. And Christ is not simply a stage in a progression, but a sharp disjunction, a reversal of the tendencies of human history, like the cataclysm he anticipates. As Paul puts it, Christ crucified is a stumbling-block and foolishness. Maybe we have to speak of the intersection of the ultimate, the infinite and the universal with the penultimate, the finite and the particular. The question of 'ending' demands some sense of a story that is not confined to earthly history.

So is it in some sense really a 'spiritual' story clothed in 'earthly' dress? That such a view was the outcome of a typological and allegorical approach to scripture is scarcely surprising. Extremists like the Gnostics asserted it was only a spiritual story, the historical and earthly dress being no more than symbolic. They were resisted, but modern scholars have always suspected that they were not resisted successfully, that exegetes like the Third-Century Alexandrians Clement and Origen were more Gnostic than they knew. In *Allegory and Event*[1] Richard Hanson explores the range of Origen's exegetical techniques with insight and thoroughness, but ultimately rejects Origen's entire approach because he utterly lacked any sense of history, and therefore had no real community of understanding with the Bible. In the light of the previous section such a judgment must surely be called into question. Yet the ancient church itself had misgivings about Origen, and our suspicions are far from laid to rest. The problem with reducing the earthly detail to symbols of a different order is that it is reductive: like other procedures we have noted, it is liable to have the effect of 'flattening' the text, this time to one basic theme endlessly repeated with rather boring regularity.

Origen believed that his procedures were justified by words of the Apostle Paul himself, frequently referring to eight par-

1. SCM, 1959.

ticular texts: Romans 7:14; 1 Corinthians 2:2,10,12,16; 9:9–10; 10:11; 2 Corinthians 3:6,15–16; Galatians 4:24.[1] All these he took to imply the necessity of allegory, because 'the Law is spiritual', and 'the letter kills, but the spirit gives life'. So the details of the text contain difficulties precisely to alert the reader to the necessity of probing further and discovering the spiritual realities to which the letter points. This is certainly not exactly what Paul meant: when we speak of attending to the 'spirit' not the letter of an agreement we are probably nearer the mark! But despite the actual outcome in developments typological and allegorical which make us feel distinctly uncomfortable, there is in Origen's position an appropriate instinct: if the Bible is the Word of God, its truths are not limited or defined by the human language which is its inevitable vehicle; if the Bible bears witness to God's revelation, that revelation is not contained solely within the 'events' behind the narrative, any more than in the text itself.

In fact Origen took the particularities of the text with the utmost seriousness, more seriously than many a modern interpreter: he was fascinated by such questions as where the refuse went in the Ark! He was the first scholar to try and sort out the wording of the text and establish a critical edition, and the first to produce systematic commentaries on the majority of books of the Bible. Despite many passages where he seems to take an exclusively 'spiritualising' view, there is much to suggest that Origen's basic understanding of Holy Scripture was 'iconic' or 'sacramental'.[2] If sometimes he seems to reduce the bread and wine of the sacrament to a mere vehicle for the spiritual Word of God, he never eschews the bread and wine, or the divine accommodation to the limitations of earthly creatures. The creation is good. Its purpose is redemptive. God uses the created order to communicate at an appropriate level with those he loves and seeks to save. Scripture too has its body, soul and spirit in the letter of the text and its moral and spiritual meanings.

1. Ronald E. Heine, 'Gregory of Nyssa's Apology for Allegory', *Vigiliae Christianae*, 38 (1984), pp. 360–70.
2. Patricia Cox, 'Origen and the Witch of Endor: Toward an Iconoclastic Typology', *Anglican Theological Review*, 66 (1984), pp. 137–47.

The letter matters because the 'material' vehicle is indispensable, just as the physical sound is indispensable to the spiritual language of music. Origen may have been a bit ambivalent about the 'flesh', but he did not in the end see it as anything other than the good provision of a merciful Father for the discipline of his wayward children, and the 'letter' of scripture belonged to the same order. The divine Logos could only be communicated through human *logoi* – in the end, only through being incarnate in human nature, able to speak with a human voice in a human language with the particular constraints of a particular human culture.

So Origen has in a sense an incarnational or 'Two Natures' view of scripture which could affirm the human words of the text as the divine mode of communication, as the vehicle indispensable to the Word of God if he were to accommodate himself to our level so that communication could happen at all. That kind of theology of Holy Scripture could potentially take historical criticism with the utmost seriousness, and in the next chapter we will turn to the 'constraints of the score', the necessity of philological and historical scholarship to establish the limitations of potential meaning. In the following chapters we will turn to the search for the 'higher truths' of doctrine and spirituality, which historical criticism has found difficult to accommodate. The problems and potential of typology and allegory will confront us again.

But before we proceed, let us gather together our thoughts on the sharps and flats of the Christological interpretation of scripture. Subjecting scripture to Christ had the effect of flattening the texture of scripture, ironing out the humps and bumps, the contrast and dissonances, and it failed to highlight Christ's fundamental disjunction from human aspirations, values and expectations: the cataclysmic newness of the End was 'domesticated' so as to reduce the tension with its climactic fulfilment of human destiny. Christ became both theme and finale, leaving little room for variations in between, and in practice, it must be admitted, Origen's exegesis endlessly and boringly repeats the theme over and over.

But what are the full implications of Origen's view of 'divine accommodation'? Surely the effect of it should have been the opposite, allowing for endless variations, so that, paradoxically, the very finality of Christ as the embodiment of that accommodation necessitates open-endedness. For if the divine Logos accommodates himself to one culture, why not to others? Why should not secular readings of scripture be appropriate, indeed indispensable, if the Logos is the universal principle of rationality? If Christ is the key to a theme repeated and varied in the biblical story, namely the pattern of divine intersection with the particularities of human history, with its variety and dissonances, its repetitions and divergences, can we exclude the possibility of other instances of divine accommodation? What about other faiths?

So if we have to do justice to all the rough and tumble of biblical variety, its ups and downs, its harmonies and dissonances, without flattening the texture of theme and variations, why not all the contrasts and contradictions of life, the dissonances as well as the harmonies, all the rough and tumble of our penultimate existence in a less than Christian world, including the existence of other faiths, and indeed the sense that Christ fulfils all human aspirations and yet is profoundly disjunctive, challenging those aspirations as we experience them in human history? I doubt if we can be true to the text without living in tension between finality and open-endedness, without allowing for contrasting shades, changes of key, antithesis and recapitulation. Christ may be the theme of Christian scripture, but the variations are multiple beyond our imagining, and he is the ending yet not the ending. And since as yet there is no final ending to the story, Christian readers need to respect readings that proceed without such a key.

5

The Question of Criteria

... we must not assign too definite *ideas* to musical compositions: this means longing, etc., this means etc. etc.
(Bayard Taylor's experience with Wagner's music: one of
the party said it meant moonlight, another sea, another so
and so, etc. etc. . . . .) . . . Music is vague: purposely so. This
is no objection. If it is, the Bible must fall. The Bible
furnishes a text for every creed. The Mormon allows you
to have twenty wives, and furnishes you good authority
from the Bible, while the old George Raff and his Harmon-
ists (and the Catholic priest) allow you no wife, and give
you good authority from the Bible: the slaveholder draws
his warrant from the Bible, the abolitionist draws *his* warrant from the Bible: the Unitarian proves from the Bible
that there is but one person in the Godhead, the Trinitarian
that there are three. Arnold reads the plain and lucid statements of St Matthew and Paul and arrives at Rationalism,
while from the more mystical writings of St John a thousand
mystagogues construct a thousand forms of belief. This is
because the Bible is so great; and it is purely because music
is so great that it yields aid and comfort to so many theories.

Those notes come from Sidney Lanier, a Nineteenth-
Century musician, composer and essayist, and was found
in *Pleasures of Music: An Anthology of Writing about Music and
Musicians*.[1] The motto at the head of the anthology is Virgil
Thomson's comment, "Nobody is ever patently right about
music." The above extract entitled *Music is Infinite* is a tantalis-

1. Ed. Jacques Barzun, Cassell, 1977.

ing expression of that perspective, drawing as it does on the post-Reformation experience that the Bible settles nothing. There can be little doubt that modern emphasis on the 'literal' meaning has a great deal to do with that experience. People who took the Bible as 'truth' had to know what it objectively 'meant'. In the hope of establishing that, they resorted to 'literalism'.

So fundamentalists claim to interpret the Bible literally, and criticise others on the ground that they do not. The irony is that they are actually less 'literal' than the biblical critics they attack, as James Barr pointed out:[1] it is precisely because they pay attention to what the text literally says and respect it, that critics feel constrained to account for contradictions and anomalies that fundamentalists prefer to explain away. But this combat seems to presuppose slightly different senses of the word 'literal', and when Hans Frei[2] speaks of 'literal reading' of biblical narrative, he means something rather different again, for it is a reading of the Bible as a whole from the perspective of a 'literal' reading of incarnation in Jesus that he proposes.

The questions we have to face include not only what is meant by 'literalism', but also whether there are 'constraints' on interpretation provided by the score, by the text itself. Many musicians would take issue with Lanier – music is a 'language' and it has 'conventions' of expression which mean that the 'literate' musician can discern appropriate meaning: there are not 'infinite' possibilities because of the constraints of the medium.[3] Besides, the information in the score can illuminate the composer's intentions and provide some constraints: the youngster's instinct to play the chords of the Moonlight Sonata with grandeur is offset by the pianissimo marking, and obeying that transforms the nature of the statement. Surely there are similar constraints on the interpretation of scripture.

Scripture and its interpretation is the subject of the final book

1. *Fundamentalism*, SCM, 1977.
2. *loc.cit.sup.*
3. cf. Deryck Cooke, *The Language of Music*, OUP, 1959.

of Origen's *De Principiis* (On First Principles).[1] Scriptural proof from prophecy he inherited and espoused, but felt he had to defend the interpretative methods by which it was arrived at, largely because it was rejected by both Jews and heretics (notably Marcion and the Gnostics). It is those opposed to the truth who in Origen's view adopt a *literalist* interpretation. What does he mean by 'literalism'?

Firstly, he accuses the Jews of failing to recognise their Messiah because they expected the prophecies to be fulfilled in a sensible and visible manner: Jesus had not visibly built the city of God, or caused the wolf to lie down with the lamb. 'Literal' refers to actuality in the physical world. Then he accuses the heretics of attributing much in scripture to the Demiurge rather than the more perfect Deity revealed by the Saviour because they take realistically the statements about God's anger and jealousy, and can only refer these to an imperfect and unbenevolent God. "Now the cause . . . of the false opinions . . . appears to be nothing else than the not understanding Scripture according to its spiritual meaning, but the interpretation of it *according to the mere letter.*" Origen proceeds to outline the typological and prophetic approach as more satisfactory. 'Literal' means the obvious, earthly meaning which cannot allow for poetic analogy or metaphor.

Most modern Christian 'literalists' would surely eschew this kind of literalism: they know that scripture is not inviting them to worship a standing stone when it says 'God is my Rock', and much of the language belongs to 'simile'. Yet some do take the visions of Revelation 'literally', expecting the 'rapture' of the saints; and many take God's wrath 'literally', expecting vicious judgment on everyone but themselves. The difficulty lies in the spectrum of language: where do you draw the line between the 'letter' and simile, metaphor or analogy? In a sense, that is a question of theological judgment, and

1. The text is found in the GCS series ed. P. Koetshau; ET G. W. Butterworth, SPCK, 1936: this conveniently translates the Greek original where it exists, alongside the Latin translation of Rufinus, which alone provides a complete text.

only the external 'framework' brought to the text makes possible the drawing of the line.

But it is also a matter of becoming more sophisticated in our awareness of the way language works.[1] We can identify a 'gate' as a certain kind of object in the real world: different cultures may make different styles of gates, and there may be in our experience a range of sizes and types, but even so we have a clear idea of the notion of 'gate' and we regard that as the 'literal' meaning of the word. But as soon as a scientist uses the word 'gate' as a technical term in the context of a model of physical reality, the word is subtly changed and yet not changed: it is in a way 'metaphorical', a 'simile', and yet in a way 'literal' rather than 'poetic'. Perhaps it is best described as 'analogous'. So is much religious language. Origen was clear that scriptural language was not simply 'concrete', and to take the language of the Bible 'literally' was for him to empty it of all transcendent reference, to confine it to the 'corporeal' world. Allegory was required to give the biblical text appropriate depth and density of meaning.

This becomes clear as he spells out his theory of interpretation, a theory he believes grounded in the scriptures themselves. Proverbs 22:20–21 speaks of 'portraying them in a threefold manner': 'them' Origen takes as the truths of Holy Scripture. So "as a man consists of body, soul and spirit, so in the same way does Scripture". Origen suggests that there are certain passages of scripture which have no 'corporeal' sense, where we must seek only for the 'soul' and 'spirit'. But he acknowledges that even the 'bodily' part of scripture, the "covering of the spiritual truths" is not without profit in many cases, indeed is "capable of improving the multitude according to their capacity". So despite the charge against Jews and heretics, Origen is still concerned with the 'letter' of the text, unlike the philosophical allegorists of Homer, for example.

Yet for Origen the text contains 'stumbling-blocks' at the 'obvious' level of the text, deliberately set there so that we should never think that the laws and the history constitute

---

1. A much more philosophically sophisticated account will be found in Janet Martin Soskice, *Metaphor and Religious Language*, OUP, 1985.

the whole meaning, but be provoked into deeper exploration.[1] His examples of 'impossibilities' are fascinating: it is idiotic to think of the first, second and third day, and the evening and the morning, existing without a sun, moon and stars! Or that one was a partaker of good and evil by masticating what was taken from a tree! He even mocks the idea that the devil could have literally taken Jesus to a high mountain where he could have seen the kingdom of the world – Persians, Scythians, Indians, Parthians – with the *eye of the body*. Many of us would never have dreamed of pointing out such a thing, taking it for granted that the language referred to seeing with the 'mind's eye', but given modern debates about Genesis, his rather laboured 'spelling out' approach seems less unwarranted there.

If there are 'impossibilities' in the stories, there are absurdities in the legislation of Moses: no-one would dream of eating a vulture – so why forbid it? How can a goat-stag be offered as a 'clean' beast when it does not even exist? How can someone literally sit all day without moving on the Sabbath? Origen mocks the attempts of the Jews to provide 'case-law' spelling out what they may or may not do under impossible laws like not bearing a burden on the Sabbath, so defining sandals with nails as a 'burden', but sandals without nails as not. He subjects the Gospels to the same kind of examination: the command not to strike the right cheek is absurd because everyone, except those with a physical defect, strikes the left cheek with his right hand! Origen is, of course, out to make a point, and we may lose patience: but some 'literalism' still invites such teasing.

All this does *not* mean that Origen sits lightly to the wording of the text, or the essential truth of the biblical narrative: it is perfectly clear to Origen that Abraham was buried in the double cave at Hebron; that Jerusalem is the metropolis of Judaea in which the temple of God was built by Solomon, and so on. It is also clear that certain commandments are to be obeyed, like "Honour thy father and thy mother", and "I

1. Karen Jo Tørjesen, ' "Body", "Soul" and "Spirit" in Origen's Theory of Exegesis', *Anglican Theological Review*, 67 (1985), pp. 17–30, convincingly argues that the three levels are pedagogical stages.

say to you, Swear not at all.'' The exact reader must therefore 'search the scriptures', and ascertain how far the literal meaning is true and how far impossible.

For Origen the 'whole meaning' of scripture is spiritual, but the medium is the letter of the text. He was the first textual critic, a scholar anxious to ascertain the correct wording with precision, who therefore compiled the *Hexapla*, a compendium said to contain the Hebrew and several translations. He adopted the view that every detail is significant, sometimes exploiting details in order to discover the 'hidden' meaning. In John 1:28, the reading 'Bethabara' is preferred on geographical grounds, it being nearer the Jordan than Bethany. Yet this allows an appropriate spiritual interpretation, 'House of Preparation' being a translation of the name. He probed the text, not only, as we have seen, enquiring where the refuse went in the Ark but also anxious to solve such problems as how fourteen specimens of every clean animal and four of every unclean beast were to be fitted into its reported dimensions. His solution, attributed to a learned Jew, was that the cubits were geometric and therefore all the measurements were to be squared. Origen's apparent dismissal of 'literalism' has to be set aside by this profound attention to the need for precision in relation to the letter of the text.

But now we seem to be using the word 'letter' somewhat differently, and Origen himself oscillates between various senses of the word, depending on whether he is being polemical or not. Interestingly enough, the exegesis of his great admirer, Eusebius of Caesarea, complicates the picture further by implying that the 'literal' meaning of a prophecy is the fulfilment to which it points. This perhaps enables us to see that there are several different kinds of 'literalism': one is primarily concerned with the 'reference' of the text – what the text actually *refers to* – for Origen that kind of literalism is often, though not always, appropriate; another, by taking words literally regardless of whether they were meant to be metaphorical or not, is unacceptable since it does not attend appropriately to the nature of the language; another kind of attention to the letter is vital since it is concerned with the verbal sense of the text, what the text says, what its wording is, and what those words mean.

Ironically Origen himself was accused of inappropriate 'literalism' of this last kind. A treatise *On the Witch of Endor and Against Origen*,[1] written by Eustathius of Antioch in the Fourth Century, is usually regarded as one of the first attacks on Origen's allegorical exegesis to come from the so-called Antiochene School. Certainly in one long aside Eustathius objects to the fact that Origen allegorises Moses' accounts of creation, paradise and many other things, including Gospel-narratives which Eustathius thinks should be read literally, but his point here is that it is scandalous to allegorise those things and then treat the story in question in a literal manner. For his objection to Origen's exegesis of the Witch of Endor is that Origen has made unacceptable doctrinal deductions from a verbal or lexical approach to the text, without attending to its subject-matter.

Origen has taken it to be literally true that the Witch summoned up Samuel from Hades. Eustathius suggests that the narrative logic of the text suggests that Samuel was not raised at all: rather the devil used the Witch to play upon the mad mind of Saul and induce him to believe he saw Samuel. The treatise is a series of rationalistic arguments to prove that Origen's literal reading of the text is totally along the wrong lines, and therefore his deductions about the resurrection unacceptable. Eustathius is objecting to methods which ignore the sequence of the story, the intention of the story-writer and the coherence of the narrative with the rest of scripture: the problem with Origen, whether he takes a text literally or allegorically, is that he attends too closely to the verbal level of the text, and not to its 'thrust' or subject-matter. No doubt Eustathius assumed a correlation between the subject-matter and the factuality of the narrative, but he was not primarily concerned with historicity in the modern sense, any more than Origen was.

Clearly when Origen speaks of the 'letter' or the 'literal meaning', he does not mean simply 'historically factual', but

1. Text in Migne, *PG* 18.613–673.

a range of other things, and Origen's misgivings lie with any interpretation which confines its concern to merely 'corporeal' realities, whether historically factual or physical in some other way. His analogy with the body, soul and spirit explains his fundamental position: for Origen the physical world and the physical body were provided by a good Creator as a 'school' or 'reformatory' for fallen spirits; so of course the 'spirit' was superior and gave the 'body' its *raison d'être*, and sometimes Origen seems as 'spiritualist' as the Gnostics; but neither the world nor the text of scripture was to be denigrated – for they were the vehicle of God's providential care and communication. "Let everyone, then, who cares for truth, be little concerned about words and language, seeing that in every nation there prevails a different usage of speech; but let him rather direct his attention to the meaning conveyed by the words . . ."

But in the end that did not mean refusing to attend to the precise details of the text, since the smallest jot or tittle might point to spiritual realities. The problem with Origen's exegesis is not failure to attend to detail, but failure to understand the need for criteria for distinguishing legitimate meaning, failure to appreciate that the details with which he was concerned in fact provide the constraints of the score, rather than material for imaginative speculation and eisegesis.

The Antiochene reaction to Origen is often portrayed as the rejection of allegory in favour of the literal or historical meaning. But this description can be very misleading.[1] The Antiochenes were not the precursors of modern historico-critics. Their sense of history was that of the ancients not the moderns, most of them accepted prophetic and typological meanings, and they were primarily concerned with the dogmatic meaning of the Bible. They did, however, respect the philological constraints of the score, and to that extent they shared certain methods and perspectives with modern commentators.

1. For the following section, and the previous discussion of Eustathius' work against Origen, see Frances Young, 'The Rhetorical Schools and their Influence on Patristic Exegesis' in *The Evolution of Orthodoxy: Essays in Honour of Henry Chadwick*, ed. Rowan Williams, CUP, 1989.

Ancient education was based upon study of literature. It began with learning to read, and that meant reading aloud, a process not unlike rehearsing a musical score for performance. Ancient texts were written continuously with no word division and without punctuation: reading meant recognising discrete words and construing sentences so as to articulate them meaningfully, so perhaps it is not surprising that nobody read 'in their heads' before Ambrose! Ancient texts were also hand-written, and rarely were two identical: so deciding which 'text' to read was also an essential preliminary. Sorting out the 'verbal' level of the text was learnt as part of the art of reading, and therefore was the concern of the 'grammaticus' or 'primary' schoolteacher.

Correct reading of ancient literature also required considerable linguistic scholarship. Such texts contained archaic words and forms, so vocabulary and parsing occupied the class. Perhaps it is not surprising that this provoked much interest in etymology – the ancients loved to explain the derivation and meaning of words, an art they learned in the early stage of education.

The principal aim of education was to be able to compose and deliver speeches, the key to public influence and social advancement, so learning to read also involved attention to the style of the great classics, noting appropriate choice of vocabulary or imagery to create a particular effect. Comment was required on words which did not conform to the accepted ideals – grammatical solecisms, barbarisms, foreign words – and attention to ornamental devices and figures of speech, metaphor, simile, personification and so on, was basic to discussion of the import of the text. Meaning was taken to be the effect produced on the audience, and the commentator was interested in how that effect was produced through linguistic and stylistic usage. Any educated person was used to paying attention to the 'letter' of the text, and this 'verbal' exegesis was called *methodikē*.

But the other aspect of the text that sometimes needed elucidation was its 'reference'. The allusions to classical myths, gods, heroes, legends, and histories with which ancient literature was studded, had to be unpacked for the class or they would not appreciate what the text was about. This aspect of exegesis was called *historikē*, but note that did not mean 'historical' in the modern sense. The original sense of *historia* is 'investigation', and this 'historical' exegesis covers much narrative material never thought to have been historical in our strict sense.

This reading of literature continued with the 'rhetor' – that is, in 'secondary' education, as the pupil began to write compositions and learn to declaim. Concern was now focused on the author's handling of his subject-matter, literature being analysed so as to provide models to be imitated. The author's theme was distinguished from his style, the latter being the dress in which he chose to present his subject-matter. Choosing the appropriate dress was, of course, fundamental, but the theme was the heart of the matter, and the way the author chose it, delimited it, divided it up for presentation and arranged it, was as important as the style he chose to present it in. The assumption was that the author aimed to convince, and 'rhetorical criticism' was always 'audience-orientated'. There was no attempt to trace the author's 'original intention' in our historical sense; what mattered was the persuasiveness of the matter and manner of the discourse.

The principal aims of exegesis were therefore:

1 establishment of agreement about the text to be read;
2 the construal and correct reading of it;
3 the provision of explanatory notes on language and allusions;
4 what is called 'judgment', which included rhetorical evaluation, but also the discernment of the 'moral' value of the work in question.

Such an approach to literature provided methodological constraints. True allegory was not excluded: for poets often spoke 'allegorically' and the metaphors had to be explained, while etymology produced symbolism, often of an artificial kind, and the 'moral' of the work might not be its surface meaning. But here was no wholesale treatment of texts as meaning something other than what they purported to say, a development pioneered by the Stoics and increasingly used by philosophers. Rather we find here that disciplined approach to exegesis as explanation of linguistic and literary features of a text, which has shaped the forms of commentary traditional in European humanistic culture. Modern biblical commentaries and the Antiochene reaction against Origen have both been indebted to this philological tradition. Not that Origen was not himself influenced by it – at the 'lexical' level he certainly was. And that is why some criticism of his exegesis has been unbalanced and unfair. But he did not allow the philological approach to provide constraints and criteria.

As we have seen, that was Eustathius' fundamental criticism: attending only to the verbal level of the text and making deductions from it piecemeal, Origen failed to grasp what the text was all about. Characteristic of Antiochene commentaries (and modern ones) are opening chapters or paragraphs spelling out the 'hypothesis' of the book to be studied or the passage to be treated. To understand a text, it is necessary to see the 'theme', to put words and sentences into context, to discern the overall thrust. This sense of context and flow of argument provides one kind of constraint on meaning. It is something easily lost by 'proof-texting', and even by the practice of reading the Bible only in snippets, whether as daily devotional reading or through the liturgical lectionary. The philological imperative is to resist piecemeal approaches, and to try and ascertain the divisions of the text according to its own argument and logic.

Antiochene commentaries (and modern ones) then go on to examine points of detail in the text, concentrating on things that are not clear, rather than things that are obvious. Details commented on range from discussion of alternative readings, of correct punctuation and division of words and sentences, and of the way sentences are to be construed, to consideration of problems of translation, etymologies, explanations of foreign and unfamiliar words, attention to metaphor and other figures of speech, and mini-treatises, with masses of scriptural cross-references, on the special biblical flavour of certain words or phrases. Clearly this is the *methodikē* of the schools, and on the whole, this too provides constraints, rather than fuel for speculation as it sometimes did for Origen. It measures the possibilities of meaning, and enables some meanings to be excluded. There is an objectivity about language since it belongs to the public domain, has conventional structures and consists of terms with an agreed range of reference or meaning. Most ancient commentators lacked real knowledge of Hebrew, but they did have some idea what philological scholarship was and why it was important.

They then proceed to explore allusions, the reference of the text, the context in terms of the prophet's time, for example, or the events of Paul's life. This is the *historikē* of the schools. The Antiochenes were often concerned to get the *historia* right, and we find them debating such things as whether Paul had visited Colossae or not. But for the most part their comments fail to probe very far: Chrysostom takes it for granted that the reference to a previous letter in 2 Corinthians refers to 1 Corinthians, and the person who is to be forgiven in 2 Corinthians 2 is identical with the sinner in 1 Corinthians 5. Modern critics have been more relentless in their enquiry and their challenge to superficial assumptions of this kind.

Their concern with *historia* does not imply that they had the same kind of historical concern as modern commentators. Theodore recognised that the exile was referred to by the Psalmist's words: "By the waters of Babylon there we sat down . . ." But that did not mean assigning that Psalm to the post-exilic period. Tradition made David the author, so David was prophesying. The Antiochenes usually assumed the reference was to 'facts' – unless a text was clearly intended as a fable, a parable or was metaphorical; but such reference included the future 'fact' predicted by a prophecy, a 'fact' often discerned through recognising the presence of allegorical or metaphorical language. It is quite misleading to view their work as some kind of historical criticism.

What they did recognise was the necessity of discerning the 'aim' of the text, the 'subject-matter', treating the words as so many ancients did as merely the clothing given to the 'theme'. And that brings us back to their insistence upon the technique of providing summary and paraphrase to highlight the gist of the argument. This was often accompanied by historical or circumstantial introductory material, because they, like modern commentators, recognised the importance, for understanding what the text is all about, not only of intratextual context, but extratextual context. The only problem was that for the most part, they collapsed the time-sequence: so that the prophetic denunciation of the Jews was read not only in terms of the pre-exilic context but as a contemporary word for contemporary Jews. The modern sense of historical distance was not part of their equipment. So too John Chrysostom assumed in his exegetical preaching that Paul was addressing the contemporary Church, and not just the Corinthians: he notes how Paul oscillates between praise and blame, severity and tenderness, humility and assertion, how this is part of the 'economy' of his discourse as he attempts to deal with disunity, immorality, pride and disloyalty in the Church, thus using the audience-orientated criticism of the schools to facilitate appropriate moral response from his congregation.

Still, despite this lack of historical sensitivity, the Antiochenes did have exegetical techniques which recognised the constraints of the score, and Theodore of Mopsuestia got into the same kind of trouble as modern critics have done, for such things as taking consistency of subject seriously: he denied that Psalm 22 referred to the passion, despite its appearance on the lips of Jesus in the Gospels, on the grounds that the speaker refers elsewhere in the Psalm to his sins! One feature of Theodore's approach was an insight into the radical novelty of the New Covenant, and he opposed a good deal of traditional Christological exegesis of the Old Testament because it seemed to reduce that sense of novelty – in fact, it 'flattened' out the dispensations to which scripture clearly pointed. So Theodore did refer much of the Old Testament to the past, and was consequently charged with practising 'Jewish' exegesis because of his 'literalism'. However he was merely stressing something which gave most Christian exegetes some sense of a progression in God's dealings with his creation, a sense fostered by typology.

Indeed, the Antiochene approach did not exclude typology. Theodore accepts that Jonah prefigures Jesus because the extraordinary events of his life signify by 'imitation' (*mimēsis*) Christ's rejection, resurrection and conversion of the Gentiles. Here again the Antiochenes seem to have been influenced by contemporary literary criticism, and drawn on an approach to literature very different from the fables and fantasies of allegorical interpretation. It was a commonplace that literature 'imitates' life, and can therefore be instructive, especially in the moral sphere. Ancient history writing was telling the story in order to bring out the moral and explore the interaction of fate and destiny with human politics and motivation – it was meant to be a 'possession for ever', with a moral purpose, not just a pleasing entertainment, or even a reconstruction for its own sake of events as they happened. The 'imitative' function of literature was of fundamental importance. Abiding moral truths, and therefore also doctrinal truths, could be drawn from stories because of their 'imitative' quality, and typology could be justified along these lines. Key Old Testament narratives prefigured by *mimēsis* the events of the New, and the deeds of key scriptural heroes provided examples to be imitated in the lives of Christians.

This was the basis of what the Antiochenes called *theōria*, the contemplation of spiritual truth through the texts of scripture. Most were less extreme than Theodore, and allowed more than one 'subject', as well as the traditional range of prophetic and typological meanings. Like Origen, Theodoret of Cyrus interpreted the Song of Songs as referring to the marriage of Christ and his Church. Philology provided constraints which excluded the speculations of the allegorisers, but that did not mean reading scripture as merely referring to history in our sense, or to 'this-worldly' events and realities. Scripture pointed beyond itself in being exemplary and in being the vehicle of divine truths.

The contrast between Origen and the Antiochenes is best observed by comparing typical treatments of a common text – say, Matthew's version of the feeding of the multitude. Origen takes the story as symbolical of spiritual feeding, seeing the desert-place as representing the desert condition of the masses without the Law and the Word of God, and explaining that the disciples are given power to nourish the crowds with rational food. Chrysostom turns the story into proofs of dogma and moral lessons: Christ looks up to heaven to prove he is of the Father, he uses the loaves and fish rather than creating food out of nothing to stop the mouths of dualistic heretics like Marcion and the Manichees, and he let the crowds get hungry and then gives them only loaves and fish, equally distributed, in order to teach them humility, temperance and charity, and to have all things in common. Chrysostom's interpretation is anachronistic, dogmatic and moralistic, but it respects the integrity of the story rather than making it a cypher for something quite different.

So we are left wondering wherein lie appropriate constraints. For in this case Origen's perspective is not entirely arbitrary. The associations of the feeding-story with God's gift of manna in the wilderness, and with the eucharist, together with the texts 'Man shall not live by bread alone', and 'I am the bread of life', suggests that in this case Origen's exegesis has some justification. And Chrysostom's forced moralism and disturbing anachronisms offend our exegetical sensibilities. Can we arrive at any criteria for deciding the 'plain sense' of scripture?

The 'constraint' assumed by modern biblical study is history. To pick up any introduction to the subject is to be introduced to a series of 'methods': text-criticism, source-criticism, form-criticism, tradition-criticism, redaction-criticism, literary-criticism . . . The first attempts to establish the original wording, the second attempts to probe behind the texts to the earlier sources from which they have been composed, the third and fourth try to reconstruct the nature of the material in the pre-literary oral period – the object being to get back as near as possible to the original 'event', the 'fact' behind the levels of interpretation. The fifth tries to set the finished product in its original historical context, to discern the aims and intentions of the author. The sixth can be a 'catch-all', since literary-critical methods are constantly on the change, and have embraced all those already outlined, but it too can be caught in what structuralists and hermeneutical theorists might call the stranglehold of history, concerning itself with matters of 'genre', style, rhetoric, structure and composition within the literary categories available at the supposed time of writing.

Clearly all this assumes something considerably more complex than simple 'authorial intention', but in principal it works with the same assumption: that the 'original' meaning is the 'proper' meaning. 'Sociological' study of the biblical writings simply assumes the same drive – to understand the texts in their original social context. Meaning resides in the 'original', and that outlaws eisegesis, and methods of interpretation like allegory which make the text mean something other than itself. History provides constraints on interpretation.

Modern preoccupation with historicity has been the fruit of apologetic necessity. The Reformation challenged the accretion of tradition, and sought to go back to the Bible – so stimulating a sense of the 'original' meaning as an objective standard. Renaissance and Enlightenment bred a scepticism about Christian claims, both supernatural and historical, which demanded a response. Historical investigation was the way to 'prove' that Jesus was real not a myth, and that the Bible was true. Modern biblical conservatism is as much a reaction to these challenges as biblical criticism, as evidenced by a popular book like Keller's *The Bible as History*:[1] the Bible's 'factuality' has become the crucial issue, rather than its pointing beyond itself. Critical scholarship, admitting the difficulties about the Bible's factuality, resorts to appeal to divine revelation in the process of history which produced it (from A. S. Peake and 'progressive revelation', to G. E. Wright and 'the book of the Acts of God', Cullmann and 'salvation-history', and even most recently Barton's treatment of the Bible as 'witness' in *People of the Book?*).[2] Either way history has dominated the issue of biblical interpretation, and the voices insisting that Christianity is a historical religion have been strident. The exegesis of the Fathers has been evaluated,

1. W. Keller, *The Bible as History*, ET Hodder & Stoughton, 1956.
2. SPCK, 1988.

and found wanting, in the light of this modern preoccupation with history (e.g. R. P. C. Hanson, *Allegory and Event*).[1]

Preoccupation with history has meant paying exclusive attention to the 'literal' meaning, and an assumption that the literal meaning is the reference of the text to historical events. If nothing else, our excursion in this chapter into patristic exegetical methods should have alerted us to the problematic character of the 'literal' meaning, and the deeply un-traditional character of doctrinal definitions which appeal to literalism. If we take seriously the common patristic assumption that the text of the Bible points beyond itself, then neither fundamentalism nor 'liberal' criticism can stand up to the challenge, for both are preoccupied with the 'corporeal' level of the text, with modern concerns about 'historicity'. The Nineteenth-Century challenge to the literal meaning of Genesis crystallised a process long in formation, and the sad thing is that attention to traditional exegesis could have defused that debate: the Fathers knew that human beings shared their physical nature with the animals as part of creation, and were not afraid to read the Bible in the light of current 'scientific' theory about the physical world. What was important to them was the 'iconic' or sacramental nature of the created order, as well as of the biblical narratives. Bible, body and world point beyond themselves to truths of which they are the mere vehicle.

Is it true then that the greatness of the Bible, like that of music, lies in its 'infinity' of meanings, as Lanier suggested? Is it legitimate to abandon the search for constraints, and like Origen allow a multiplicity of meanings, the possibility of everyone reading the text for themselves and making what they can of it? The recent reaction against historical criticism suggests that such a situation is not only proper but to be encouraged. A text is not confined to its original meaning but takes on new meanings as it is read in new contexts. The logic of this position leads to 'deconstruction' and 'reader-reception theory', and that means relativism must be allowed its rein. If it is legitimate for liberation theology to propose that the original meaning matters less than the way the Bible

1. SCM, 1959.

inspires 'praxis' and identification with the oppressed, why is it not equally legitimate for the defenders of apartheid to read the Bible as endorsing their views? Like the Chosen People, they entered their land of Canaan, and dispossessed the Canaanites . . . Is not God with them too?

What are the constraints that suggest one interpretation is superior to another? That particular example requires constraints at the level of 'overview', of appropriate identification with the narrative subjects, constraints on the way we can legitimately speak of the narrative text 'pointing beyond itself'. Such constraints may be difficult to establish for all readers, but within the sociolinguistic community of the Church and Christian tradition, the constraints are provided by the frameworks already discussed, and the doctrines to be discussed in the next chapter. But constraints are first required at the 'lexical' level of words and sentences, as the Fathers knew only too well.

In fact the musical analogy itself points to the fact that precision and discipline are indispensable. A good performance requires skill, skill acquired over a long period through commitment, and disciplined practice. If the notes are not precisely in tune, if the players are not co-ordinated by precise corporate discipline, the music will go all awry. Appropriate style depends on precision of 'placing' both rhythmically and harmonically. Attention to the nature of the 'language' in which the communication is taking place is vital, or muddle is the result. In other words careful scholarship at the 'lexical' level is the essential starting-point for any interpretation. The philological tradition provides that kind of precision. It can rule out 'misreading' of the text and so provides some necessary constraints, akin to the musician's discipline and precise attention to the score.

Much of biblical scholarship is concerned with this essential preliminary discipline, with attending to the languages in which the texts were written, to the precise wording of texts contaminated by copyists in the centuries before printing, to issues like the beginning and end of sentences, whether something is meant to be a statement or a question, to the discipline of translation, and the questions that translation inevitably throws up, such as valid verbal equivalents, accept-able cultural transference, equivalent speech mannerisms, and so on. Archaeology and social history inevitably make their contribution to the pursuit of what the language used actually can have meant – for language is in the public domain, and is incarnated in a society and a culture at a particular moment of history, whether we like it or not. This is not some kind of optional extra, or the dubious pursuit of modern intellectuals with a historical consciousness. It is basic to reading texts, as the Antiochenes knew. We need the experts as our servants to help us read the texts appropriately at the level of the 'letter'.

And here modern historical consciousness has made us more sophisticated than the ancients. They may have used Greek as their native language, and therefore had some advantage over us in reading the New Testament, but they were not conscious of linguistic change and development, of changing social meanings, of historical distance, nor were they so skilled in disciplined research and investigation. They fell into mistakes through anachronism which modern schol-arship can rectify. On the other hand, they sometimes provide us with important information long since lost, and some of them, like Origen, Eusebius and Jerome, were aware of the need for Hebrew, the need for 'investigation' into textual, linguistic, historical and geographical data. They were aware that the context, both intratextual and extratextual, affects meaning, and that 'biblical Greek' was in some ways a special language in itself which had to be 'de-coded' through careful lexical work. We have more sophisticated procedures because of the invention of printing, the availability of concordances, mass information technology, and so on. But many of the methods are the same, and such scholarship can settle some debates about meaning and provide some necessary precision.

Sitting loose to all this creates 'reading' problems, bad superficial performances in which sentences are misunder-stood, and conclusions drawn which are 'out of tune' with the text. A reader has to acquire a certain competence, or reading is impossible, and it is always possible to improve reading competence by practice and by further study and learning. The purpose of translation and commentary is to assist competent reading, so that 'expertise' is passed on. But that does not mean there is any substitute for the 'reader' or 'performer' having the commitment and discipline to grapple with the text, and become acquainted with the difficulties and constraints that must be imposed on performance.

False veneration of a particular translation and unwillingness to have one's biblical literacy challenged and improved, is usually characteristic of people who should know better. Disadvantaged and illiterate people who have come to take the Bible seriously have been known to make considerable personal sacrifice to learn basic reading competence, and most such people know that there is always more to learn. The Christian Bible has long since ceased to be confined to the experts: it is not left in its sacred original tongue like the Torah or the Koran. But that should not mislead us into thinking that the mediation of expertise is not an important part of the process of making the Bible available for everyone to read. Good professional performers should assist and inspire the large body of amateurs.

But over-attention to some kinds of detail may be as corrupting of good reading as was Origen's propensity to deduce spiritual meanings from jots and tittles. Much modern historico-critical method fails to grasp the 'thrust' of the text, being preoccupied with the reconstruction of events behind it or the process of composition. Many theories are highly speculative hypotheses, concerned to 'read between the lines' rather than focus on the 'subject-matter', desirous of explanation rather than exposition. Again the tradition of philological scholarship should provide constraints. A text has a 'theme': we may not be entirely happy about the ancients' tendency to abstract it from the 'clothing' of its actual language, preferring to think in terms of language actually shaping our knowledge of the world, of the 'subject-matter' inhering in the actual words of argument or narrative. We may also be aware of the many different 'overviews' or 'analyses' of a text which may be offered. But the discipline of paying attention to context and genre should provide some measure of constraint on what a text, or part of a text, may mean.

In trying to determine the flow of argument or narrative, modern scholarship has sometimes been short-sighted. The source-critics tended to assume that the biblical writers sat in studies with scissors and paste using compositional methods they might have used themselves. The recognition of the importance of oral tradition was a vital corrective. And we still have much to learn about the ancients' attitude to literature in general, unthinking the assumptions natural in society where books are two a penny. The 'aura' surrounding the written word, and the essentially 'oral' nature of literature, since like music it only 'existed' in performance, are things we find difficult to take seriously. A text was a 'linear' reality, like a piece of music, its secrets gradually unveiled through time, as the performance unfolds, depending for the communication of shape on conventional forms, on repetition and allusion, on *mimēsis* (imitation) and on the consequent *anamnēsis* (recollection) of themes, phrases, narratives, that have gone before. Recently the advent of rhetorical criticism has helped to alert us to some of these features, and our reading of ancient texts can therefore be improved.

In particular, we may now begin to discern the natural dissections of the text within its overall flow, instead of being preoccupied with what seem to us to be disunities. Such disunities and incoherences have often provided the fuel for the critics' fire, leading to suggestions about seams between sources, composite documents, and so on. We need to pay a lot more attention to whether the ancients would have seen these as inconsistencies and contradictions as we do, rather than leaping to conclusions on the basis of our own questions and analyses. A case in point is the suggested inconsistency of Paul's discussion of idol-meat in 1 Corinthians 8–10: recognition of the fact that Jews and early Christians accepted both that the idols were nothing but lumps of stone and wood, and that the daemons could use them to deceive human beings, removes the problem, and enables the reading of the text as a unity rather than a patchwork.[1]

1. See Frances Young, 'Notes on the Corinthian Correspondence', *Studia Evangelica*, 7 (1982), pp. 563–6.

Yet in this area of genre and context, the careful assembly of what evidence we have, and self-conscious disciplined comparative study of ancient literature, has led to greater sophistication than the ancients had. Greeks read translations of Hebrew texts as if they were like their own literature: the case of prophetic oracles has already been noted. Again our advances are due in some measure to modern concern about anachronism, as well as interest in questions of authorship and origin. Historical awareness has helped to provide proper constraints.

This is true too in relation to narrative: the 'interpretative' process inevitably involved in producing a narrative went largely unremarked in the ancient world, and even where they took note of different versions, they rarely raised critical questions about which was closer to the facts – Herodotus just assembled the different stories he collected side by side. If a unitary version was preferred the tendency was to 'harmonise': so Tatian composed his harmony of the Gospels, the *Diatesseron*, while Irenaeus sought to justify placing four versions side by side. Some, like Eusebius, sought to 'solve' the problems, usually resorting to harmonistic suggestions. Historical criticism is a necessary corrective, and often refines the philological methods which provide the necessary criteria and constraints for interpretation. For it is a refinement of the discipline of paying attention to the reference of the text. Some account has to be given of why Jesus is reported to have died at Passover in the first three Gospels, but on the Day of Preparation in the Fourth Gospel, unless we are prepared simply to gloss over what the text actually refers to.

Despite its apologetic origins and its preoccupation with what lies behind the text, historical criticism refines the essential procedures of philological method, just as musicological research illuminates appropriate performance through the search for historical authenticity, and just as a performer attends to what the right notes are, what might be the right style of performance and ornamentation, and so on. As precision and discipline are important to musical performance, so attention to the 'letter' of the text matters because it can provide the necessary constraints on interpretation. Neither Bible nor music is infinite at the 'lexical' level.

But the 'lexical' level is only the 'corporeal' or 'physical' vehicle of the real subject-matter. What about the way both Bible and music relate to the listener and 'point beyond themselves'? Does anything do here? Against Lanier, it must surely be affirmed that it is only when we get the precision right that we can appropriately be drawn into the music, or the text, so that it illuminates our own experience. Furthermore, it is not possible for either the performer or the informed audience to make what it likes of music, because it too has its conventional language, as Deryck Cooke has convincingly shown. Something is being communicated. So too, if the Bible is the vehicle of divine revelation, something is being communicated, and the listener cannot make it mean anything he or she likes.

The language of music depends on a set of conventional 'signs' and 'motifs', like sequences of notes, use of certain keys, which have been built into the tradition, and are consciously or unconsciously replayed in the creative imagination of the composer. These are communicated by the performer and recognised by the practised listener. They belong to the 'community' of music-lovers versed in the tradition. So too the 'spiritual' language of scripture is not without constraints, and is heard within the community attuned by practice to recognise the conventions and respond to them. Typology and allegory are written into the texts, whether we like it or not, and biblical *mimēsis* rings true to its repeated 'themes'. It also rings true to life: for great literature is never pure 'escape' from the real world, and the 'pointing beyond itself' includes the illumination the text brings to our existence. The process of discerning that true to life *mimēsis* is assisted by liturgical *anamnēsis*, the replay of what is familiar, in the reading and performing of scripture, in the sacraments of the church. It is to such discernment that we turn in the next chapters.

6

The Bible and Doctrine

The words of the Bible, like the sounds of music, convey a content. That content is intimately related to the medium – indeed indistinguishable from it, and communicable in no other way. What is that content?

In the case of music, as in the case of the Bible, the issue has been much debated. Deryck Cooke's precise analysis of musical language was written at a time when there was much talk of 'pure form' and 'pure sound' being the essence of music. He showed that music was a form of communication, and what it communicated, through its structures and tonality, was the composer's emotion. The meaning therefore lay in the 'intention of the author' to express his feelings, the initial inspiration of music being the natural expression of those feelings in a melodic or harmonic shape, which was then refined naturally or laboriously by the technique or conscious compositional skill of the composer.

Cooke's thesis has an immediate plausibility: music of all styles and cultural contexts has included keening lament and joyful dance, it has expressed tribal celebration and communal anguish, and it is evident it still does as television enables us to share 'Rhythms of the World'. Clearly even 'pure classical' music expresses or creates feelings of joy, fun, sadness, poignancy. Cooke was giving analytical substance to a basic instinct, but one particularly associated with the Romantics, whose emotional music ranges from the 'lightness' of a Mendelssohn to the dark passions of a Berlioz. Saint-Saens suggested that music cannot convey purely abstract ideas, but it

is all-powerful when it comes to expressing the several

degrees of passion, the infinite nuances of feeling . . . Music takes up where speech leaves off, it utters the ineffable, makes us discover in ourselves depths we had not suspected, conveys impressions and states of being that no words can render. That is, incidentally, why dramatic music has so often been able to get along with mediocre words . . . it is music that creates the whole; words take second place or become actually needless.[1]

But those words of Saint-Saens themselves suggest that to confine the meaning of music to the conscious feelings of the composer is to limit it. Music itself 'creates' response, and expresses 'meanings' which are inarticulate. In the centuries before passion was desired and respected, when feelings were seen as destructive and negative, certain kinds of music were frowned upon for that reason, but music and chant still found its place in worship: why? Because it could express a 'passionless' response to the world and its Creator. Music meant order and harmony, it reflected

the musick of the Sphears: for those well-ordered motions, and regular paces, though they give no sound unto the ear, yet to the understanding they strike a note most full of harmony. Whosoever is harmonically composed, delights in harmony . . . There is something in it of Divinity more than the ear discovers: it is an Hieroglyphical and shadowed lesson of the whole World . . . In brief it is a sensible fit of that harmony, which intellectually sounds in the ears of God.[2]

The somewhat parallel view of scripture in the writings of the early Christian philosopher Clement of Alexandria is striking: for him religious literature of its very nature consisted of 'hieroglyphs' and riddles shadowing the divine reality. Both music and scripture have an 'imitative' quality which means their content may go way beyond the conscious feelings or responses of author or composer.

1. From Barzun, *op.cit.*
2. Sir Thomas Browne, from Barzun, *op.cit.*

The great modern theologian Karl Barth listened to Mozart every morning before beginning work. He did not share Mozart's conscious beliefs as a Freemason, and he thought Mozart's lifestyle "leading a rather frivolous existence", but for Barth, Mozart's music had become the vehicle and expression of pure praise, because "he knew something about creation in its total goodness that . . . (no theologian) either knows or can express and maintain as he did". One significant thing for Barth was Mozart's instinctive communication of the perception that "the sweetness is also bitter and cannot therefore cloy", and that "in its totality, creation praises its Master and is therefore perfect". There is a sense in which music enabled Mozart to transcend his own immediate feelings, and reach beyond himself to an unsurpassed perfection of musical form and harmony embodying and communicating a content he could never have articulated, creating a response in himself and in others that could happen in no other way. Yet his music is pure Mozart, and could be the music of no other. That is the paradox. Mozart "simply offered himself as the agent by which little bits of horn, metal and catgut could serve as the voices of creation, sometimes leading, sometimes accompanying and sometimes in harmony . . . He himself was only an ear for this music, and a mediator to other ears."[1]

So the 'content' of music is controversial not because it has no content, but because the content is so bound up with its form of expression that articulating it in any other way is impossible. Nor is it appropriate to confine the meaning or content to the composer's intention, or to grand passions. A concert performance of *The Marriage of Figaro* highlights the point: on stage the music succeeds in lifting the farce into a profound exploration of human relationships, broken and reconciled; but without the action the music both implies and yet utterly supersedes the foolish plot, having a content more 'sublime' than words can describe. Great music is 'there' beyond the self of composer, performer or audience, just as God is 'there' beyond the projections and images of human conceptuality, the words of the Bible, the performance of the

1. *Church Dogmatics*, III.3.50.

preacher, the reception of the congregation. Yet the divine communication, like the content of music, is inseparable from the medium of communication, whether it be the created order, the text of the Bible, the person and words, actions and sufferings of Jesus, the sacraments and the life of the church, or experience of the Spirit. (For surely in Christianity, all of these and not just one or the other act as means of communication).

Because 'the medium is the message', at least in the sense that the one is inseparable from the other, biblical revelation must be taken to reside in some sense in the words of scripture, and not in events behind it. The content of God's communication is the revelation, his Word, and the medium of that communication is the text and language of the Bible. His activities and his self-disclosure are now 'incarnated' in the words which enshrine the memory and witness, and those words, despite lending themselves to inappropriate piecemeal interpretation, provide some constraints on meaning, even though they can never exhaust the meaning of the communication.

The truth of that communication does not depend on precise correspondence between the 'historical facts' and the reports of the biblical witnesses, any more than it depends upon the ability of limited human language to express the inexpressible. Yet ultimately the content cannot be separated from the form of expression, though it transcends it. That is why attention to the text is vital. But that is also why the sociolinguistic community to whom the text belongs has never been able to refrain from deducing 'doctrine' from the text, trying to spell out the content in ways that are grasped more readily. The difficulties involved in this are not dissimilar to the difficulties involved in spelling out the content of music, and Lanier's conclusion that both are 'infinite' is not without some justification. But the content of both, their ability to 'imitate' reality, communicate truth and evoke response, remain discussable, and the discussion often produces clarification, despite the elusiveness of agreement.

Doctrine has arisen out of debate, debates which have attempted to define the content, to deduce from the text the truth enshrined in the meaning of scripture. But such deduction constantly takes on a life of its own, and needs 'correction' from the text. Philological method has rightly challenged traditional doctrinal frameworks: for such frameworks inevitably affect the way scripture is read, and may be distorting – they have certainly caused the Christological 'flattening' discussed earlier, and against which there has been justifiable reaction. If, as we noted earlier, systematic theology is an inevitable consequence of trying to understand what scripture is about, we must now observe the necessity of debate about an appropriate systematic theology.

All doctrinal constructs are attempts to express the content of the various forms of divine communication in another medium so as to correlate bewilderingly diverse material and arrive at some conception of truth. But as in the case of music, the content abstracted from the original medium is elusive, and different interpretations are the inevitable result. A performer's understanding of the music to be performed will be affected by the constraints of the score, by beliefs about the composer's intentions, and by an understanding of the proper content of musical communication. In the same way the biblical interpreter cannot help being affected by doctrines accepted or rejected as valid expressions of the content of scripture, as well as by appropriate philological constraints together with the refinements of historical criticism. But that does not mean adopting a view of the Bible's 'infinity' which is effectively a dispirited relativism. It means a commitment to discussion and debate: for there is content, and the content, however elusive, is the truth of God.

The basic doctrinal impulse was to try and spell out what God is like on the basis of his revelation. For Marcion and the Gnostics the God depicted in the Old Testament could not be God, and the debate about God's nature was first bound up with the debate about the contents and unity of scripture itself, as we have seen. At that stage the unity of God and the coherence of the biblical delineation of his nature and purpose were the primary objects of discussion.

Paradoxically, the very effort to establish the unity of God led to a view of his nature and activity that could seem to threaten that unity. God's 'Word' or Logos, though internal to himself as his Thought or Reason, was 'projected forth' as the instrument through which the transcendent Father created and revealed himself, in a way similar to the manner in which our spoken statements are the 'projections' of our thoughts. This Logos spoke by the prophets, and was then incarnate in Jesus. But was he not now an entity other than God the Father, though deriving his being from him? The Modalists, like the Adoptionists, were probably reacting against this 'Logos-theology' when in their different ways they reaffirmed the unity of God. Since the scriptures affirm one God and only one God, either Jesus must be a 'mere man' 'adopted' as Son by the one God, or the one God appeared in different modes, as Father, Son and Spirit. All of these 'theories', Logos-theology included, were different ways of deducing doctrine from the text of scripture, and all could appeal to scripture for their justification. It was assumed that revelation meant revelation of God's being and nature, and that such information was the subject-matter of scriptural texts.

In order to trace how scripture was interpreted when doctrinal debate caused appeal to texts, we will examine Tertullian's treatise *Against Praxeas*.[1] 'Praxeas' clearly represents a Modalist, despite the difficulty in determining precisely who the nickname (= 'Busybody') represents. Tertullian, like other anti-heretical writers, assumes his opponent is inspired by the devil, but acknowledges that the devil himself can come jolly near the truth. Eventually he tells us the scriptural texts on which the Modalist case is based:

I am God and beside me there is no other (Isa. 45:5)
I and the Father are one (John 10:30)
He who has seen me has seen the Father . . . I am in the Father and the Father in me (John 14:9–10)

How does Tertullian deal with what seems to be a plausible case on the basis of these texts?

1. Text ed. and tr. E. Evans, SPCK, 1948.

The intratextual argument emphasises the inadequacy of an interpretation which highlights a few texts and makes many others subordinate to them: the proper course, suggests Tertullian, is to interpret the few in the light of the many. So in discussing the last of the three, he adduces many Johannine passages which show that the Son is the Father's Commissioner, and that it is in the light of the perspective of the Gospel as a whole that this particular text must be understood. The Son represents the Father, and so "he who has seen me, has seen the Father"; all things are delivered to the Son by the Father, and in that sense "I am in the Father and the Father in me". The very form of the text "I and the Father are one" implies two beings which are related to one another, and the whole Gospel narrative points to a divine 'economy' in which the Father is in heaven, the Son on earth, the Father receiving the prayers of the Son, and making his promises from heaven. This implies distinction rather than separation, Tertullian suggests, but even if it did mean two separate gods as the opposition kept insisting, it would still be better than "so versatile and changeful a God as yours". According to Praxeas, the Father proceeded forth from himself and returned to himself. The argument has shifted to extratextual theological considerations.

To arguments of this type we will return, but to stay with arguments based on overall context first, we should note that for Tertullian the intratextual argument is not confined to the immediate context in the Johannine Gospel, but to the scriptures as a whole. The other Gospels point to the same distinction between Father and Son, and the Isaiah passage cannot be taken in isolation. Of course there is no God but God, but that does not mean there is no Son of God: according to Proverbs 8, Wisdom says, "When he prepared the heaven, I was present with him," and so "He stretches out the heavens alone" does not mean 'without Wisdom', who is the Son. Rather the word 'alone' is meant to exclude the heretical view that various angels were involved in constructing the world. When he says "I am God and there is no other beside me", he does not need to add "except my Son", anymore than the sun would say, "I am sun and there is no other beside me

117

except my ray". Again intratextual argument gives way to an extratextual argument by analogy.

Looking at such scriptural arguments what is evident is that Tertullian can exploit the complexity of statements in the scriptures against a simplistic exegesis of a few key texts, but to make any sense of that complexity he has to resort to rationalistic arguments deriving from outside scripture. The treatise is full of scriptural reference, but the force of that reference lies in a number of features which originate outside the text.

In a sense the very form of Tertullian's treatise is an acknowledgement of this. He begins with the Rule of Faith, a summary such as we met in Chapter 3. He assumes that this is a summary of the biblical revelation, and that scripture is to be interpreted in the light of it. In other words he brings to the text a traditional 'framework' of interpretation which he sees no reason to question. He then spells out in a rationalistic way what this Rule of Faith implies with respect to the question at issue: the only way to believe in One God is to respect the mystery of the divine 'economy' by which the Unity is distributed into a Trinity. The opposition's assumption that this means division is all wrong. He insists on distinction without separation, and proceeds to suggest that the 'monarchy' is not divided if an emperor shares sovereignty and government with his son. Such an argument is easily backed up with proof-texts like 1 Corinthians 15:24–28, but the basis of the argument is analogy rather than scriptural authority (and one cannot help wondering whether Tertullian is exploiting the potential of the opposition's favourite word in a slightly unfair way: deriving from *archē*, which, having the alternative meanings 'rule' or 'beginning', had long been the term used for the 'first principle' in discussions of the origin of all things, the Monarchians could have been focusing on the unity of God as first principle, rather than upon his monarchy in the sense of sovereignty).

From exposition of the proper understanding of the Rule of Faith, Tertullian turns to an explanation of the 'Logos-theology', misunderstanding of which he wishes to defuse. Logos-theology certainly had its roots in a particular understanding of scripture reached by correlating, justifiably or not, certain key passages from both Old and New Testaments. Tertullian exploits all these eventually, but basically he argues 'rationalistically'. As we can hold internal conversations with our Thought or Reason, so could God. He thus developed his Ideas, and the divine Intelligence appears in scripture as his Wisdom, which is clearly stated to have been present with him when he prepared the heaven (Prov. 8:22ff). This Word or Logos, under the name of Wisdom, was begotten as God's Son, according to the scriptures: "My heart has emitted my most excellent Word" (Ps. 45:1) is correlated with Psalm 2:7: "You are my Son; today I have begotten you." This begetting took place when God said "Let there be light". Later Tertullian explains that at these words, immediately there appears the Word, "that true light which enlightens everyone coming into the world". Indeed, it is the Johannine Prologue which confirms all this, but again it takes argument external to the texts to establish that this Logos or Son is 'real' rather than a 'void, empty and incorporeal thing'. Further arguments drawn partly from proof-texts, but also from naturalistic analogies, establish that the 'prolation' of the Son does not mean a separation, a fragmentation of the divine, like the emanations of the aeons in Gnosticism: God sent forth the Word as the root puts forth the tree, the fountain the river, the sun the ray.

So building on the traditional Logos-theology, Tertullian argues towards a Trinitarian view of God in which the 'economy' is not threatened by the 'monarchy', but rather upholds it. Then he challenges the opposition to adduce "proofs out of scripture as plainly as we do". The rest of the treatise is a fascinating collection of arguments in which philological and rationalistic techniques are used to show that many texts are absurd if they are read with the 'framework' of Modalism, but clear if interpreted according to the models Tertullian has expounded. In the process the peculiar difficulty of the 'anthropomorphisms' of the Old Testament is given an explanation coherent with Tertullian's theological model of what God is like: God is invisible, and Moses could not see him and live; yet God spoke with him face to face, and many others, Abraham, Jacob, Isaiah, Ezekiel, are supposed to have seen him. How? What they saw, though in a glass darkly, was the Son, visible as being derived from God – one cannot look at the sun, but one can endure a ray because it is a 'derived' portion. The Son, even before the incarnation, was 'rehearsing', 'learning' to converse with human beings. Because the Son makes the invisible God visible, he receives the titles of God himself, standing as God in relation to men: the two are in fact one. The alert reader should have spotted the scriptural elements in that argument, but they are interwoven with a process of correlation and deduction which exploits human logic.

How far does doctrinal argument of this kind depend on taking the scriptures 'literally'? A brief review of the ground covered should reveal that the issue of literal or allegorical by-passes what is going on completely. At one point Tertullian pays too much attention to the letter of the text, exploiting the plural in the creation-story, "Let us make man in our own image", arguing for God having a conversation with an associate, and so failing to attend to the possible linguistic phenomenon of the 'Royal We' (as we refer to it in English). He is more philologically sound in rejecting the interpretation of Genesis 1:1 (found in Irenaeus, for example) which misread the Hebrew *bara'* as the noun for 'son' rather than the verb 'create' and translated: "In the beginning God made for himself a Son." But overliteralism is a recurrent problem: despite his attention to context when it suits him, he can ignore it and take the precise wording of a text according to the letter, as in the case of Psalm 45:1, which was quoted above as referring to the emission of the Word from the heart of God, yet, given the parallel clause, should refer to the Psalmist's heart overflowing with his 'goodly theme'. On the other hand, he properly pours scorn on the heretics who separate 'Jesus' and 'Christ', making the latter refer to the Father: it is linguistically incorrect since 'Christ' signifies 'Anointed', and describes one anointed by the Father. Generally Tertullian assumes a straightforward reading of the 'plain sense' of the texts he refers to, but the assumed 'reference' of the texts often depends on Christian tradition, and is not clearly literal,

120

typological or allegorical: into which category goes the fundamental assumption that Wisdom in Proverbs 8 refers to the Logos who is the pre-existent Christ?

In fact the criteria for interpretation are based on (1) the Rule of Faith or tradition; (2) rationalistic deduction and logical argument, sometimes using valid philological points; (3) prior theological assumptions, like the changelessness, invisibility and passionlessness of God. It is simply blasphemy to suggest that the Father suffers or is crucified, and no justification of this theological axiom is necessary. In fact, however, Tertullian turns to scripture to substantiate his claim: "My God, my God, why hast thou forsaken me?" was uttered so as to prove the impassibility of God, who 'forsook' his Son, so far as he handed over his human substance to the suffering of death. The intention of scripture has become the exclusion of false doctrine! Is that really true to the texts of the Bible? If not, were these early interpreters on completely the wrong track in thinking the 'content' of scripture was revelation of God's nature and being?

Tertullian concludes by accusing his opponents of holding a doctrine close to the Jewish faith – that is, "so to believe in One God as to refuse to reckon the Son besides Him, and after the Son the Spirit". The 'content' of the New Covenant is taken to be belief in Father, Son and Spirit as both Three and One only God. As this kind of understanding was refined in later debates, the recognition grew that God's nature and being is an ultimate mystery, for he is infinite and incomprehensible. Indeed, that very perception justified the need for revelation. Discussion of the content of that revelation, however, continued to illuminate the way in which simplistic deduction of doctrine from a few key texts could impoverish the scriptural revelation by confining it to too precise theological definitions. Arianism was a clear case in point, especially in its extreme Eunomian form. To imagine God was definable was to limit him. The complexity of his revelation could not be confined to inadequate doctrinal formulae, if only because the message is ultimately inseparable from the medium.

What Tertullian was working towards, with the complex evidence of the Gospels as his most convincing material, was something like a Trio Sonata, a musical statement 'grounded' in the bass or 'continuo' played on cello and harpsichord, but gloriously elaborated in the interweaving melodies of two superimposed instruments, the whole being a perfect unity yet all three parts being distinguishable by the attuned ear. God the Father, the one God of all the monotheisms derived from the Jewish scriptures, is the ground or bass common to all doctrinal systems; but Christian tradition hears that bass as underlying the melodies played by the Word and the Spirit, the whole comprising the 'content' of the biblical revelation.

In detail modern exegetes would find it difficult to accept all Tertullian's arguments: some are, as we have seen, philologically unsound or pay insufficient attention to context; others depend on anachronistic readings; others conflate texts from different genres, or correlate texts in ways that seem without obvious justification. We may also feel that scripture is not about this kind of thing, and other doctrinal deductions are just as plausible. Yet Tertullian cannot be faulted for drawing attention to the wider context of particular texts, and seeking to do justice to the complexity of the evidence. It has been the mind of the Church, and not without justification, that any Christian conception of God has to grapple with a drama that has a single providential plot involving three actors, distinguishably yet inseparably involved in the process of communicating with the human race and persuading human beings to respond and receive the benefits of that single divine outreach. Such a mystery would seem to represent something of the complexity of the revelation implicit in scripture. Trinitarianism has the richness and harmonic complexity of a Trio Sonata, and that very richness gives it greater potential to represent the text in its fullness, given that the 'content' is ultimately not separable from the biblical means of expression, and all doctrine is an inadequate 'second-order' expression of the divine communication.

So in Christianity, the doctrine of the Trinity serves as a working-model of the content of the divine revelation: but we must beware of suggesting that it is stated so explicitly that failure to read it in scripture is morally culpable. Jews and Muslims rightly bear witness against Christian tendencies towards tritheism, and within the Christian matrix, Unitarians and Oneness Pentecostals remind us that a tritheistic Trinitarianism must ever and again be corrected by their well-reasoned and scriptural case against it. Debate about the content of the divine communication can never be finally closed this side of the End.

In the programme of chamber music performed by the early church, the various movements of the trio sonata were followed by a duet. Some wanted a solo with accompaniment, but two instruments, each with their own properties, were eventually allowed to play together in such a way that their contrapuntal melodies were united in one whole piece.

It was examining a text from the Fifth-Century Christological controversies which first alerted the present writer to the inappropriateness of using the categories 'literal' and 'allegorical' to analyse the use of texts in doctrinal debate. Such debates focused on the appropriate meaning to be attributed to the language of scripture, and proceeded, as we have seen, in rationalistic ways, with appeal to extratextual theological assumptions and intratextual cross-reference. Since the Alexandrians and the Antiochenes, the contestants in the Christological controversies were also in contention about biblical interpretation, the Antiochenes consciously opposing the allegorical procedures of Origen, it is the more interesting that doctrinal debate did not elicit disagreement over texts in the Old Testament assumed to be Christological and interpreted in symbolic ways. In fact the process of doctrinal formation developed a set of ecclesiastically agreed symbols which became the basis for a refined allegorical treatment of scripture, so that dogma and spirituality were not divorced and spirituality was 'disciplined' by the 'orthodox' understanding of key texts.

The first dialogue of Theodoret's *Eranistes* provided a case-study.[1] The Antiochene viewpoint is put on the lips of 'Orthodoxus', the Alexandrian on those of the 'Carpet-bagger' (that

1. Frances Young, 'Exegetical Method and Scriptural Proof – the Bible in doctrinal debate', *Studia Patristica*, forthcoming; text ed. G. H. Ettlinger, Oxford, 1975.

is, Eranistes), and the implication is that Antiochene Christology is right. It is perhaps not surprising, therefore, that the Alexandrian character often seems rather weak and inconsequential. Nevertheless the dialogue represents arguments on both sides which are found elsewhere, and each has recourse to their respective favourite proof-texts found in other controversial literature of the period. It seems reasonable to use it as a representative sample for our purpose of examining the use of the Bible in doctrinal controversy.

The crucial debating point is how to interpret "The Word became flesh": what does 'became' mean in such a context? The contestants have already agreed that Father and Son have a common 'being' or 'essence', and yet each has a particular individuality. They have also agreed that the attribute *atreptos* (unchangeable) belongs to the common divine essence. So the issue is how to take John 1:14 without attributing change to the Word.

Eranistes is reluctant to accept either of the alternatives presented: that the Logos underwent change or 'seemed' to. Nevertheless he insists that the Logos was 'enfleshed'. His opponent demands to know the meaning of such a word: does it mean 'took flesh' or 'changed into flesh'? Eranistes is not happy with either substitution, and appeals to the word of scripture, justifying his perplexity with "all things are possible to God". Orthodoxus agrees that the Creator can do what he likes with his creation, but suggests that he cannot change his own nature, since he is 'unchangeable'. Proof-texts are adduced for each point. "One must not investigate hidden matters," suggests Eranistes.

The appeal to mystery is the last resort of all theologians when the going gets rough, yet Eranistes' position is not without legitimacy. What he wants to say is that the language of scripture should be taken seriously, but it cannot mean exactly what the words mean in ordinary human language since the object about which scripture speaks transcends such language. Gregory of Nyssa had already wrestled with this problem in discussing what it means to speak of God having a Son: the idea must be purged of all crude physical and sexual connotations, yet that does not mean that the language

124

has no real meaning and content. It is not a question of whether the words of scripture are to be taken 'literally' or not, but a question of the substance and signification of religious language, a question of the appropriate content or reference of human vocabulary when it refers to a being not confined to the created order and not ultimately definable. Eranistes justifiably insists that the word of scripture be attended to and not emptied of meaning, yet to press it in the literalising way of his opponent is to distort the mystery of the divine reality: "The manner of his enfleshment escapes me," he pleads, "but I have heard that the Word became flesh."

Orthodoxus then suggests that the way to understand biblical language is to read it in the light of scripture's own linguistic usage elsewhere. Eranistes remains reluctant to substitute any other phrase, but now Orthodoxus is justified: exegesis has to proceed either by searching for substitutes or by paraphrase so as to be able to say 'this' means 'that'. He proposes to understand 'became' in John 1:14 in the light of "he 'took' the seed of Abraham" in Hebrews, and "he 'took' the form of a servant" in Philippians. A fundamental method of exegesis is cross-reference. Many differences of interpretation are in fact the result of disagreement about what constitute appropriate cross-references. Orthodoxus extracts from Eranistes agreement that the Apostle is just as inspired as the Evangelist, and therefore his procedure has justification; but modern exegetes might feel less confident that Paul can be used to understand the Johannine Gospel in such a simplistic way.

So far then we have observed a rationalistic discussion of the meaning of a word used in a particular scriptural text which proceeds partly on the basis of prior theological axioms, partly on the basis of philological techniques such as cross-reference. As Orthodoxus tries to lead Eranistes to adopt his conclusion, he uses a number of subsidiary arguments, all based on scriptural interpretation since Eranistes is determined only to attend to scripture. Amongst these figures an appeal to Genesis 49:10ff. Both contestants agree that the reference to the sceptre not departing from Judah implies the incarnation, and taking that as the starting-point the following verses are given allegorical interpretation so as to become Christological, and this allegory is promulgated by the Antiochene!

The Greek text reads: "His presence (*parousia*) the nations (*ethnē* = Gentiles) expect; he washes his own garment in wine, and his own veil in the blood of the grape." The Epistle to the Hebrews justifies taking the 'veil' as the 'flesh'; and the text is associated with "I am the vine", and the flowing of blood and water when the Saviour's side was pierced. Clearly Genesis 49.11 is about the eucharist: "for as we call the mystical fruit of the vine after the holy blood of the Lord, so he named the blood of the true vine the blood of the grape". From allegory we move to 'type' or symbol, but this is not meant to be "merely" symbolic, a figment of the imagination. The visible symbols – bread, wine – are honoured by the names 'body' and 'blood' – not "changing their nature," says Orthodoxus, but "adding grace to nature". Clearly the language of Genesis 49:11 is not dissimilar to eucharistic symbolism. It actually refers to the Lord's body. Allegory it may be, but it denotes an important reality through sign, through symbolic language. This is the true meaning of the text, a meaning on the basis of which doctrinal deduction is possible. And both sides find it acceptable.

Eranistes represents those who wanted a solo with accompaniment rather than a duet. As he discerns where Orthodoxus' argument is leading he protests that the implication of 'taking flesh' is a doctrine of 'Two Sons'. Orthodoxus retorts that to speak of the God–Word changing into flesh does not produce one Son – it just produces flesh! Eventually the two sides would find a rapprochement at Chalcedon, though suspicion and reservations lived on. The unity of a duet is not immediately evident when the protagonists emphasise the difference of the two parts. What is evident in the process of debate is the attention each was giving to appropriate methods of deducing meaning from scripture. The following points seem clear:

1. The effect of debate was not to produce an appeal to the 'letter' or a resort to literalism, but rather an increasing awareness of the nature of religious language, and the need for sophistication in arriving at appropriate meaning. The proper procedure for such an undertaking is the search for equivalents, and rational discussion about the applicability of ordinary assumptions about meaning to the entities referred to in the text. Such debate about meaning required, and still requires, theological reflection and not just historical research.

2. The search for equivalents or suitable paraphrase proceeds on the basis of cross-reference, and differences in interpretation are usually to do with decisions about which cross-references are relevant and valid. There was a tendency to regard the language of scripture as so much a unity it could be indiscriminately appealed to. Modern exegetes, because of their sensitivity to different authors and genres, are often more wary of cross-reference than the Fathers were. But testing scripture against scripture is an indispensable procedure if doctrinal content is to be deduced from it.

3. A great many unquestioned assumptions about meaning lie in the background of the discussion. Many texts were taken to have a 'self-evident' meaning which made it possible to refer to them to prove a point without discussion. Many of these unquestioned assumptions involved an agreed set of symbols, types, prophecies, and so on. As in the case of cross-referencing, modern exegetes often feel qualms about the assumption of these interconnections, and would hesitate to make deductions from them. But this may be to impoverish our sensitivity to allusion and to special nuances built up within a religious tradition.

4. The assumed reference of the text is what most obviously determines its meaning. But that reference may be obscured by metaphorical and symbolic language. Certainly the Fathers accepted that the proper reference may be what the text, assumed to be prophetic, appears to predict. Such reference was thought to be just as valid a basis for doctrinal deduction as any other. The most notable case in point,

though discussion has not arisen from the *Eranistes*, is the universal assumption in patristic exegesis that Wisdom in Proverbs 8:22ff is to be identified with the pre-existent Christ. When the interpretation of this text became problematical as a result of the Arian controversy, that fundamental assumption was never challenged. Rather the difficulties were circumvented by referring the problematic words to the incarnation: that was when "he created me". The consequence was very convoluted allegorical exegesis of the passage. Be that as it may, such a universally assumed reference is not itself 'allegorical' or 'typological' or 'literal' – in other words the traditional categories do not assist us in describing what is going on.

5. Metaphorical language clearly lies on a spectrum. At one end it can be taken as virtually 'literal', though not straightforwardly so when it refers to divine realities. At the other end, it may be entirely 'allegorical', words being used to refer to something quite other than their own proper content. In between is a whole range of symbolic, typological and mystical meanings which are not merely symbolic but have real significance. One might almost suggest that a correspondence theory of language has to give way to some kind of sacramental understanding of how language functions. This is no less the case when texts are being used to deduce doctrine.

6. Philological method provides the rational tools for determining meaning, but judgment is required when using them (for example in agreeing what cross-references are valid), and certain crucial moves depend on extratextual axioms, whether theological assumptions or traditional frameworks. This is why some modern exegetes have misgivings about patristic scriptural proof. But the real implication for the Bible and Doctrine is that philological constraints are themselves subject to the constraints of the rationality operative in the cultural context within which interpretation takes place. Doctrine can only be read from the Bible within the closed world of the Church's Salon, and even there the context in terms of the rationality operative at any one time has been subject to radical shifts over the centuries.

So the Duet (One Christ in Two Natures) and the Trio Sonata (One God but Three 'Persons') were composed on the basis of deductions from the text which sometimes proceeded in ways that no longer convince, yet these models still provide the patterns of performance for those gathered within the privileged chamber of Lady Church. It is hardly surprising that debate about their implications continues. They are 'second-order' 'models' attempting to define what has been revealed about the nature and being of One who is transcendent. They are an attempt to spell out the content rather than attend to the medium of the divine communication in its bewildering complexity. Yet they seem to remain the best way of focusing performance of the texts in so far as they can be regarded as doctrinal communication: alternatives always over-simplify and reduce the harmonic richness.

Christian doctrine has been deduced from scripture through argument and assumption, rational debate and symbolic insight, through attending to philological constraints, to contexts immediate, intratextual and intertextual within the canon, and by justifying the results by appeal to mystery, sometimes more appropriately than at other times. The Christological reading of Old Testament texts explored in an earlier chapter played a vital role, contributing to fundamental assumptions about reference from which deductions could be made. Scripture, tradition and reason worked hand in hand to produce doctrine.

But the crucial question is: does all this doctrinal formulation really constitute the 'content' of the biblical revelation? Did the assumption that the texts revealed what God is like distort the perception of what the revelation really imparted? Does the Bible introduce us less to God's Being than his character and actions (a point recognised by the Fathers themselves when they said God was unknowable in his essence, but known in his activities)? So is it basically narrative, the story of God and his people? Does it point to a 'salvation-history' into which we can be drawn? Does it reveal God's will and purpose? Is it better understood as 'law' with a kind of legal binding force, or as 'resources' for understanding our human predicament? Does it inspire our human spiritual pilgrimage, or give us a blueprint for Christian moral and social action? What is the 'content' communicated by the Bible, and what kind of 'authority' does that suggest the Bible might have over our lives, as individuals or as a Church? To put it in more conventional terms, has concentration on the faith to be believed, on objective doctrine (*fides quae creditur*), submerged the faith whereby belief is reached, that which evokes faithfulness, the subjective response to God's grace worked out in life (*fides qua creditur*)? Would it be more appropriate to concentrate on the Gospel-message of salvation as the content of the biblical revelation, rather than doctrinal formulations?[1]

Such a challenge is not only inevitable but proper. Since the Bible consists of many different genres, it is not in any case appropriate to flatten out its content to one kind of communication, as we have already suggested earlier. As in the case of music and drama, the debate about what kind of thing is communicated can go on endlessly. It may help our reflections to consider what is involved in any act of communication, especially artistic communication, and the models analysed by the ancient rhetoricians are sufficiently sophisticated to provide a good starting-place.

Effective communication or 'persuasion' involved three kinds of 'proof' (*pistis*): the first essential was 'ethical' conviction, which meant, not what we mean by ethical, but rather the credibility of the speaker based on his *ethos* or character; the second was 'pathetic', which again did not mean what we might suppose, but rather appeal to the feelings and emotions of the audience, eliciting reactions which would fuel appropriate response and decision; the third was 'logical', which meant the seeming force of the argument, the apparent convincingness of the subject-matter, the effectiveness of the content of communication. The proper level of style, adopted in the light of the material and the context in which the

1. *Scriptural Authority and Narrative Interpretation* (in honorem Hans Frei), ed. Garrett Green, Fortress, 1987.

communication was taking place, gave appropriate expression to the dynamics of the interchange.

Christian faith (*pistis*) involves trust based on convictions about the character of God demonstrated in his words and works. It involves the response of 'being persuaded' by God's communication, thus being led to conversion and conviction, assent to what seems the truth, and decision to act in accordance with the will of the divine persuader. The message communicated, or the 'content', must involve some sense of the identity, character and activity of the God who addresses people, as well as the proclamation of his call, his will and his promises, so it will involve some measure of narrative, some measure of doctrine, some measure of 'law', some measure of assurance – all kinds of 'arguments' and information to bring about 'persuasion' to respond. The 'subject-matter' is therefore intimately bound up with the very act of communication. It is not surprising that the roots of the Christian understanding of faith have been traced to the process of persuasive rhetoric, the Greek word *pistis* being at home in both contexts, and meaning 'faith' or 'proof'.[1]

But in the case of God's communication, there is a further element, namely the 'mediation' of human communicators, the 'authors' of scripture, the 'performers' of scripture. In a sense, these, like Mozart, "simply offer themselves as agents by which little bits of horn, metal and catgut (or rather Hebrew and Greek script) could serve as the voices of creation (or of God) . . ." Yet both 'composer' and later 'performer', despite submitting themselves to be spokespersons of another, remain essentially themselves. Watching Tortelier play Haydn, one is struck both by the complete submission of the artist to the music being performed, so that he himself is simply 'delighted' and totally unselfconscious, and by the projection of the performer's own personality, which has to be there to 'win' the attention of the audience, and without which the performance would be flat and uncommunicative. So a preacher infected with the exuberance of the Word of

1. James L. Kinneavy, *Greek Rhetorical Origins of Christian Faith*, Oxford, 1987.

God communicates not himself or herself, and yet the self is essentially bound up in the act of communication. The divine communication necessarily involves 'Two Natures': justice has to be done to the human element in the 'mediation' of God's Word.

And the communication takes place in many different cultural contexts, many different ages, and that affects the process of communication as much as the three classic forms of 'proof'. Inevitably performance is affected both by the context and by the consequent audience reaction, not just by those factors noted at the start of this chapter, namely the constraints of the score, beliefs about the composer's intentions and understanding of the proper content of musical communication. Indeed the 'content' is so bound up with the process of communication, including its reception, that it will necessarily 'change': a basic continuity may be fostered in the socio-linguistic community to which the texts primarily belong, but shifts in perspective and emphasis, as well as revision and challenge provoked by new readings of the texts, will inevitably modify the whole communication process, and so produce shifts in what is perceived to be the content. To hazard a very broad generalisation, one might suggest that in the post-Reformation Church, the Bible has been read less as providing information about the internal arrangement of a Trinitarian God, and more as offering the truths necessary for salvation.

A more comprehensive account of the communication process along such lines will honour God's present use of the texts as much as the process whereby the texts came to be.[1] The content of the communication will not be confined purely to doctrine, or law, or narrative, or spiritual resources, but all these things and more. And the authority of the Bible will be perceived as neither intrinsic to it nor simply accorded to it by the believing community, but as lying in its persuasive and converting power, its ability to evoke the response of faithfulness by communicating the address of One who is worth trusting.

1. Wood in Green, *cit.sup.*

The Church's 'chamber music' helps the mind to attend to some of the music being performed, because compared with a full orchestral fantasy, the melodies and harmonies of Trio Sonatas and Duets are more accessible to the analysing ear. The architecture can be grasped and the results are intellectually satisfying, indeed exciting and stimulating. They certainly evoke response. But a fully persuasive performance of the Bible requires attention to other musical genres, to a larger ensemble of players. Large-scale music has the power to awaken the listener and command attention, and the effect of the Bible is not unlike the impact of compulsive sounds which can energise, which an audience cannot help participating in and being changed by. Just as music conveys not just intellectual satisfaction but emotional stimulation, so the response of assent needs the response of 'exultation' and 'passion'. Naturally, we turn next to the Bible and Spirituality.

7

The Bible and Spirituality

Open to me, my sister, my love, my dove, my perfect one: for my head is full of dew, and my locks with the drops of the night (Cant. 5.2). Our interpretation will help you to grasp the meaning of this text. Moses' vision of God began with light (Exod. 19:18); afterwards God spoke to him in a cloud (Exod. 20:21). But when Moses rose higher and became more perfect, he saw God in the darkness (Exod. 24:15–18).

Now the doctrine we are taught here is as follows. Our initial withdrawal from wrong and erroneous ideas of God is a transition from darkness to light. Next comes a closer awareness of hidden things, and by this the soul is guided through sense phenomena to the world of the invisible. And this awareness is a kind of cloud, which overshadows all appearances, and slowly guides and accustoms the soul to look towards what is hidden. Next the soul makes progress through all these stages and goes on higher, and as she leaves below all that human nature can attain, she enters within the secret chamber of the divine knowledge, and here she is cut off on all sides by the divine darkness. Now she leaves outside all that can be grasped by sense or by reason, and the only thing left for her contemplation is the invisible and the incomprehensible. And here God is, as the Scriptures tell us in connection with Moses: *But Moses went to the dark cloud wherein God was* (Exod. 20:21).

Now that we have considered this, we must examine how our text is connected with what we have said. The bride used to be *black* (Cant. 1.4), when she was darkened with obscure doctrines. And then the sun shone, the sun that warms the seeds cast rootless upon the rocks by temptation. She has been overcome by the powers that war within her; she has not kept her vineyard (Cant. 1.5); and because she did not understand herself, she has led herds of goats to pasture instead of sheep. But when she has torn herself from her attachment to sin, and by that mystic kiss she yearns to bring her mouth close to the fountain of light (Cant. 4.15), then does she become beautiful, radiant with the light of truth, having washed away the dark stain of ignorance.

She is compared to a steed (Cant. 1.8) because of the speed of her progress, to a dove (Cant. 2.10) because of the agility of her mind. Like a steed she races through all she perceives by sense or by reason; and she soars like a dove until she comes to rest with longing under the shade of the apple tree (Cant. 2.3). That which overshadows her the text calls an apple tree instead of a cloud. But then she is encompassed by the divine night (Cant. 3.1) during which her Spouse approaches but does not reveal Himself.

But how can that which is invisible reveal itself in the night? By the fact that He gives the soul some sense of His presence, even while He eludes her clear apprehension, concealed as He is by the invisibility of His nature. What then is the mystic initiation which the soul experiences during that night? The Word touches the door (Cant. 5.2); and by the door we may understand man's reason in its search for what is hidden; it is through reason that what we seek can make its entrances. Truth, then, stands outside the door of our souls, because we merely know *in part*, as the Apostle says (1 Cor. 13:12), and knocks at the door of reason with symbols and mysteries, saying: *Open*. And by his urgent message He suggests how we must open the door, by handing us certain keys, that is, the beautiful words of our text, by which we may open the lock. (Gregory of Nyssa, *On the Song of Songs*, 11)[1]

1. Quoted from Jean Daniélou and Herbert Musurillo, *From Glory to Glory*, New York, 1961, pp. 246–8: text in the Jaeger edn, *Gregorii Nysseni Opera*, vol. VI, *In Canticum Canticorum commentarius*, ed. H. Langerbeck, Leiden, 1960.

According to Gregory of Nyssa, the content of the Song of Songs is an account of the mystical ascent of the soul to knowledge of God, and he goes on to explain what the 'keys' are, how 'the drops of the night' are connected with the dark night of the soul described earlier, how the locks are the Prophets, Evangelists and the Apostles ... As the passage indicates, he has already suggested that the *Life of Moses* is really about that too. What scripture is about is a certain kind of understanding of life's journey, and the Word is the persuasive plea of the divine lover searching for response. The paradox lies in the fact that the passionate language of erotic love is meant to win the soul to a passion beyond passion.

Such an understanding of the content of the divine communication in scripture depends upon reading the Song as allegorical through and through. In fact the place of the Song in the canon demanded an interpretation other than the straightforward carnal view that it was a love-poem attributed to Solomon, and Jewish interpretation had long spoken of it as the Song of Israel's Bridegroom, God calling to his Beloved. Origen had 'baptised' this basic idea, taking it to be the Song of the Word to his Bride the Church, but also to the soul of the individual seeker after truth. It is this tradition which Gregory follows and develops, and it remained the approach to the Song throughout the medieval period, and beyond. Only the rise of historical criticism undermined such an approach.

The use of the Bible in spirituality seems to demand some kind of allegorical view, because it requires a method of reading 'ourselves' into the text. The view that the content of the Bible was doctrine might allow the reader to withdraw his or her subjectivity, to accept or reject that revelation 'objectively' and without personal involvement, just as historical criticism seems to permit an 'objective' reading of the texts as historical evidence. Yet the texts themselves seem to demand response, and the question is: how? How does their performance effect communication? How is 'audience participation' stimulated? Do we need to reclaim the allegorical tradition to ensure effective identification with what is going on in the world of the text, so that it meaningfully affects our lives?

The way in which literature, music and drama 'teach' or 'involve' the audience is a much discussed question, from ancient times into the present. Clearly emotional involvement is an important element, but so is identification with the characters or the situation represented. 'Representation' or *mimēsis* (= imitation) was one of the key concepts in ancient literary criticism, and since this was clearly important also in typological approaches to scripture, we may find some useful clues by turning to Aristotle's discussion in the *Poetics*.

According to Aristotle, *mimēsis* is common to all art, including music. Roughly speaking the term means 'representation': a picture represents its subject, an actor represents a character, a play represents an action, event or story. In a sense they are all 'fictional', images, representations or simulations of real human life. For this reason, Plato had referred to poetry and drama as 'lies' or falsehood, and had criticised the poets' claim to teach. Aristotle is more prepared to explore the possibility that, as everyone assumed, literature and drama had a moral importance, and could represent truth. One of the deepest problems about biblical interpretation is the fact that people have not recognised that the Bible has both the limitations and potential of all other literature. Many suppose that either it must all be factually true or there is no truth in it: that is a false alternative based on insensitivity to what art is all about, whether arising from the sheer naïvety of those who used to write letters to Mrs Dale, or the narrow sophistication of the philosopher who spurns literature.

For Aristotle, poetry – and he is particularly concerned with its dramatic form in tragedy – may "offer material which, if not describable in terms of truth, can at any rate be argued to make some contribution to the understanding of human realities".[1] The subject-matter of tragedy is people in action: "poetic *mimēsis* represents, and dramatises, human life in its

1. *The Poetics of Aristotle*, tr. and commentary Stephen Halliwell, University of North Carolina Press, and Duckworth, 1987, p. 73.

essential aspect of purposive, ethically qualified action".[1] Aristotle suggests that such mimetic activity is natural, children 'playing' at life from their earliest years, and 'imitating' life in their models and drawings. It is part of the process of understanding to engage in such mimetic activity.

The dramatist does this on a heroic scale. He is not dealing with the particulars of history, but with 'universals', and so it is not a matter of direct realism. The unity of plot which Aristotle seeks is a kind of abstraction of the action from all the complexities of the everyday, all 'sub-plots', so highlighting a 'typical' dilemma. Tragedy in ancient Athens was more like modern opera than stage-plays or cinema: the *mimēsis* was 'larger than life', the figures 'heroic', and the story familiar in advance. By the selection of the plot and its particular representation, the 'action' was clarified, and embodied "factors of more general validity" rather than "matching individual reality".[2]

For Martha Nussbaum[3] the interplay of 'luck' and human motivation is the substance of what Greek tragedy is about, and in Aristotle's ethical philosophy she finds a parallel exploration of the complexity of the 'good life'. As Aristotle suggests, tragedy is neither about the moral giant nor the obviously wicked: rather it explores the vulnerability and fallibility of one esteemed and prosperous. The reversals and recognitions of the plot are supposed to arouse pity and fear in the audience, an effect only possible if the 'dilemma' 'rings true', if it could happen, if in some sense the spectators are able to sympathise or 'identify' with the situation, though "tragedy is a *mimēsis* of human beings better than ourselves" (*Poetics* 15).

Throughout his discussion Aristotle is concerned to show that the various elements of tragedy which he distinguishes – plot, style, music, character, thought – are meant to arouse pity and fear, and in his initial definition of tragedy (*Poetics* 6), he throws out a comment never fully explored but the source of endless discussion since: ". . . through the arousal

1. *ibid.* p. 76.
2. *loc.cit.* p. 108.
3. *The Fragility of Goodness*, Cambridge, 1986.

of pity and fear effecting the *katharsis* of such emotions". The emotional impact of poetry was another fundamental reason for Plato's criticism of it, and his attempts to subject emotion to reason left a legacy the early Christians would exploit. Modern psychology has deplored this suppression of emotion, and imagined that Aristotle was suggesting significant things about the therapeutic effect of experiencing emotions often denied. This seems to be reading far too much into the text, though it would appear that Aristotle thought there was "more to be gained by educating the emotions than repressing them".[1] Nussbaum suggests that *katharsis* simply means 'clarification', basing the claim on its usage elsewhere in philosophical discussion.[2] Within a religious context, the word means 'purification', and Greek drama originated in a religious festival, so that may be more significant than some have allowed for.

Whatever conclusion may be reached about the implications of *katharsis*, the emotional impact of tragedy was clearly approximate to that of opera, and any discussion that takes no account of that is bound to be wide of the mark.[3] Aristotle does not explicitly discuss the role of the chorus, and says little about the music. But "much of the emotional effectiveness of classical drama seems to have resulted from the music and dancing". The feelings of the audience were evident in their reactions, and the chorus often expressed and stimulated those reactions of disgust and protest, pity and compassion, dread and fear, which the action was supposed to produce. The performance was meant to stimulate participation and involvement at the emotional level. Such emotion could be described as 'ecstasy' or *enthousiasmos*, a kind of possession by divine madness.

The Greek theatre originated in a religious festival: it marked a great occasion and corporate expectation, group

1. John Jones, *Aristotle and Greek Tragedy*, Chatto and Windus, 1962, p. 21.
2. *loc.cit.* pp. 388–90.
3. W. B. Stanford, *Greek Tragedy and the Emotions*, Routledge and Kegan Paul, 1983.

dynamics such as operate at a football match. Aristotle would like to emphasise the 'cognitive' element in poetry, and undoubtedly the audiences looked for ethical instruction from the plays. But in suggesting that reading a tragedy is as good as going to a performance, he perhaps underestimated the impact of performance itself, especially when music was a key component. As we have seen, music communicates 'feeling'. Like the persuasive orator, the dramatist wanted to stir feelings in response to his communication. He was engaged in *psychagōgia* – 'leading the soul' – and that process of *psychagōgia* in tragedy has been understood as

> something like this: the complex, co-ordinated movements of rhythm, voice-melody, instrumental music, dance, gesture, imagery and story drew the 'souls' of the audience into its 'song' . . . As the drama gathered momentum to its climax, like a flooding river it drew their jangling thoughts, feelings and sensations into its controlled current and harmonised them in its flow. Once the climax was passed and the drama's movement gradually grew quiet, the audience was quietened with it . . . in harmony of the whole 'soul', all disturbance (*tarachē*) removed . . . for a while.[1]

So the art of communication involves stimulating audience reaction, and audience involvement is created through *mimēsis* and through deliberate activation of emotional responses to events. *Pathei mathos*: learning comes through suffering, through feeling:

> There is a kind of knowing that works by suffering because suffering is the appropriate acknowledgement of the way human life, in these cases, is. And in general: to grasp either a love or a tragedy by intellect is not sufficient to have real human knowledge of it . . . The exploration of such conflicts through our own *pathē* as spectators, our own

1. Stanford, *loc.cit.*

responses of fear and pity, is supposed to provide us with, and to help to constitute, just this sort of learning.[1]

Even without the development of allegorical interpretation, the use of the Bible in spirituality has been possible because of the different mimetic qualities of the Bible's different genres. It is this which allows the intratextual world to impinge on the extratextual world and the extratextual world to be taken up into the intratextual world. The narratives are 'larger than life' and so 'clarify' the lives we have to live by becoming 'universal' rather than simply belonging to the particularities of history. At the same time we are drawn into the action by identification and reflection, or into the confession and praise of the Psalmist, or into the crowds around a prophet, a wisdom-teacher or Jesus himself. Stories become exemplary, parables a direct challenge.

The simplest case is the use of psalms. Athanasius, the intrepid defender of the Nicene Creed in the Fourth Century, wrote a letter to Marcellinus on the interpretation of the Psalms. It begins by suggesting that the Psalms contain in embryo everything the scriptures contain: the creation, the patriarchal narratives, the exodus, the history-books, the prophetic writings, the coming of Christ – all are there in the Psalms, and the grace of the Spirit is common to all the biblical literature. But there is a difference:

> In the other books, those who are reciting what the saints are saying or what is being said about them are proclaiming what has been written about these holy ones, but the listeners are well aware of themselves as other than the saints about whom the word is spoken; and when certain actions are commanded, the hearers may go so far in reverence and zeal as to imitate the saints. However, in . . . the psalms, it is as if one's own words were being recited; while those who listen to the words are pierced to the heart and appropriate to themselves what is expressed in the songs as if the words were their very own . . .

1. Nussbaum, *loc.cit.* p. 46.

It seems to me that the psalms are as a mirror in which you contemplate yourself and the movements of your soul, and thus confess your understanding of them.[1]

Athanasius then lists suitable psalms for various circumstances in life or various spiritual moods. He continues:

... it is very necessary not to pass over the reasons why words of this kind are intoned with melody and song. For there are certain simplistic people among us who, while they believe that the words are divinely inspired, yet consider that the psalms have been put to music merely for the pleasure of the listener. But this is not the case. For Scripture does not seek just for elegance and sweetness for its own sake, but rather it is composed in such a way to be of benefit for the soul.

There are two reasons in particular. First, it is fitting that the divine Scripture praises God not only in the single tone of prose, but also by the whole range of the voice ... The second reason is this: just as the concord of sound of flutes played together results in a harmonious unity, so too when the various movements of the soul are recognised, that is the reasoning faculties, and the desire and the passions in the soul, and the activity of the members of the body originating in these movements, the reason does not wish that a man be in disharmony with himself, nor be alienated from himself. Consequently it is best to act according to reason, but worst is to act according to the passions ...

Lest any disturbance of this kind occur in us, reason wishes the soul to have the mind of Christ ... to take advantage of this guide and by it to take hold of the faculties of sensation in the soul, and to direct the members of the body towards obedience to reason. As a plectrum in music, so one becomes a harp, wholly attentive to the Spirit, that one may obey through all the members of the body and

1. Quoted from *Early Christian Spirituality*, ed. Charles Kannengiesser, Fortress, 1986; text in Migne, *PG* 27.11–45.

the movements of the soul and may serve the will of God. The harmonious recitation of the psalms is an image and a model of this kind of calmness and tranquillity of the faculties of reason . . .

For the praises to God on well-sounding cymbals, the cithara, and the ten-stringed harp again symbolize the natural concord of the members of the body like the harp strings, while the reasoning faculties of the soul become like cymbals . . . by the rhythmic melody the soul is well ordered and forgets its passions, and fixing its gaze upon that mind in Christ, it concentrates its faculties on that which is most excellent.

So the emotions were to be educated and purified, as in tragedy, and this was effected through the use of music. This aided identification with the psalmist, a kind of being taken out of oneself, what the ancients would call 'ecstasy'. The musical performance of the text of scripture was enough to effect this *katharsis*. However, it was through preaching, through the transfer of rhetoric from the schools to the basilicas that the divine communication became most persuasive.

What happened as the Church conquered the Roman world was the substitution of the scriptures for the classic repertoire made up of Homer and the dramatists. People like the Cappadocian Fathers in the Fourth Century and John Chrysostom, the 'Golden-mouthed' preacher of the early Fifth Century, communicated the content of the Bible as rhetoricians had communicated the old stories and poetry of classical antiquity. Biblical characters became heroes celebrated in panegyrics, displaying the classic virtues. Rhetoric, just like drama, aimed to create response, to stimulate the feelings and emotions of the audience. It was the art of persuasion. Long before in the Second Century, Melito had already exploited its techniques to arouse pity and fear as he retold the story of the deaths of the first-born in Egypt. Now the Cappadocian Gregory of Nazianzus makes the Easter events contemporary:

Yesterday, the lamb was slain and the door-posts anointed,

and Egypt bewailed her first-born, and the Destroyer
passed us over . . . Today, we have escaped from Egypt,
and from Pharaoh, and there is none to hinder us from
keeping the feast to the Lord our God . . . Yesterday I
was crucified with him; today I am glorified with him . . .
yesterday, I was buried with him; today I rise with him
. . . (*Orat.* 1)[1]

One *mimēsis*, namely the traditional typology of Passover, is
enhanced by another *mimēsis*, as the story of the past becomes
the present story of actor and audience, and the reality being
lived is meshed with the 'action' of the text.

Chrysostom, the pastor and preacher, recognised the pastor
and preacher in St Paul; the paradoxes of authority and love,
discipline and persuasion, evident in Paul's relationship with
the Corinthian church, are mirrored in Chrysostom's relationship with his congregation. So there was no problem in understanding the text as both 'historical' and contemporary. One
situation was the *mimēsis* of the other, and the 'gap' was closed
by empathy. Constantly Chrysostom read between the lines
to bring out the tone of Paul's voice and his use of tactics to
win over his hearers. He re-created for his hearers a drama of
pastoral handling, observing the way Paul oscillated between
praise and blame, mixed severity with tenderness, humility
with assertion. He notes that Paul's initial praising of the
Corinthians in his Second Letter is not very close to truth,
and explains that Paul praises them *oikonomikōs* – out of tact,
preparing the way for reproofs to come. Paul's subtle handling
of the Corinthians in their disunity, immorality, pride, disloyalty, and so on Chrysostom regards as part of his loving
care – one minute he scares them, next he softens his words
to win them. Now this rhetorical creation of a pastoral drama
produces direct communication with Chrysostom's congregation – he has no need to be explicit about drawing morals.
The empathy of Chrysostom the pastor with Paul the pastor
produces a creative but non-explicit interplay between the

1. Text in Migne, *PG* 35; ET NPNF Series II, vol. VII.

two different audiences who, by implication, share the same shortcomings.[1]

Similarly, Chrysostom's congregation is expected to find the praises of the Psalmist exemplary, and so make the words of the Psalms its own in the way Athanasius made explicit. Thus his Homilies on the Psalms[2] areintended to catch up the congregation into the world of the text. On Psalm 9, he suggests that God is worshipped in song and celebration. It is impossible to see him – so the prophet composes songs, communicating with him through the songs, kindling his own desire, seeming to see him, and even through singing songs and hymns, kindling the desire of many others. The Psalmist is like a lover; for lovers are always like this – singing love-songs when they cannot see the loved one. Praise comes from thinking the things of God, his wonders, what happens day by day to individuals and to people in general, the marvels of creation. The worshipper gets his materials from everything – heaven, earth, air, beasts, seeds, plants, the law, grace – there is a whole sea of blessings to be told. God's goodness, his *philanthrōpia* (love to humanity), his great salvation is the source of rejoicing. On Psalm 42, the image of the lover is again exploited, this time the lover drooling over anything connected with the absent loved one: so the worshipper loves God whom he cannot see, by contemplating his creation, and by associating with God's dear ones, those saints who are close to him. Chrysostom dwells on the beauty, greatness and goodness of God, evoking a sense of elusiveness, and yet stimulating the congregation to love of him despite his being inconceivable: "God speaks of the love of birds for their young, the love of fathers for their children, the tenderness of mothers, not because he only loves like a mother loves her child, but because we have no greater proofs of love than these examples."

Homiletic material shows how the rhetoricians of the

1. From Frances M. Young, 'John Chrysostom on First and Second Corinthians', *Studia Patristica*, xviii, pp. 349–52. Texts in F. Field, *Ioannis Chrysostomi interpretatio omnium epistularum Paulinarum*, Oxford, 1845–62; translations are available in *The Library of the Fathers*, Oxford, 1840ff.

2. Text in Migne, *PG* 55.

Church could get a tight-packed mob in a basilica to respond
to the biblical material as a dramatist could sway an audience
in a theatre, by exploiting the assumption of *mimēsis*, and
playing on emotional reactions. The liturgy increasingly used
dramatic action and music to enhance the effect. So as the
preachers inveighed against the theatre for its lasciviousness,
the Church borrowed from it time-honoured techniques for
its own purpose of persuasion; and as intellectuals adopted the
(Stoic–Platonic) ideal of purification from passions, preachers
exploited the rhetorical and poetic arts rejected by the philosophers to create audience participation and emotional
involvement.

Christian exegetes also explored the 'universals' in the
'heroic' stories of the Bible. Cyril, the Fifth-Century Patriarch
of Alexandria, was the principal protagonist in the great
Christological controversy, but what interests us here is his
main work on the Pentateuch, entitled *On Worship in Spirit and
in Truth*.[1] Here we find not only the traditional view that the
Torah is 'type' and 'shadow', that circumcision is of the heart,
and Christ the fulfilment of the Law, but a treatment of the
Patriarchal narratives as paradigms of the 'universal' human
experience of sin, conversion through repentance and return
to a better life.

This 'universal' is narrated in the Adam-story, which demonstrates that the human race is lost without the efforts of
God's grace to recall it, and then played out again and again
in subsequent narratives of exile and spiritual famine, followed by repentance: Abraham's migration and the Exodus
are taken as paradigms of the grace of God effecting conversion. The work is not so much a commentary as a biblically-
based treatise on the human predicament and the way out of
it. The reader is drawn into this perspective on human life,
and by identification finds his own life illuminated and challenged. Rescue from the death caused by sin is foreshadowed
in the Passover and Exodus, and the journey image runs
through to the inheritance of the Promised Land under Joshua
= Jesus (the Greek form of the name). The law was given

1. Text in Migne, *PG* 68.

'for our sake', pointing to the law of love and true worship, and the conquest speaks of our spiritual warfare. The whole is a highly integrated reading of the story of redemption as the universal to which the Pentateuch points, and into which people are to be drawn.

Now Cyril was Alexandrian, and it would be easy to dismiss his work as allegorical. Yet it is fundamentally based on the *mimēsis* explicit in typology, and the notion that narratives can express 'universals'. The whole perspective is deeply imbued with traditional types rather than spiritual speculations, and the ancient sense of 'recapitulation' we found in Irenaeus is more fundamental than the kind of mystical ascent usually assumed to be outlined by such as Origen and Gregory of Nyssa. Perhaps that means they should be reassessed. For they too pursued these types and recapitulations. Furthermore Origen's three levels of scripture analogous to 'body', 'soul' and 'spirit' have recently been understood in terms of pedagogical progression rather than different orders of reality.[1] Clearly Cyril, like Origen and in typical Platonic style, conceives of realities at two levels, the realities perceived by the mind and the realities perceived by the senses. The former, the spiritual realities, are represented in the latter through signs, parables, symbols, and are discovered through *theōria*, contemplation. In otherwords the narratives provide a *mimēsis* of spiritual truth. And that implies a notion of spiritual journey, both 'universally' for the whole human race, and individually for each soul that participates in the pattern of fall, exile, famine, repentance and restoration.

So Cyril has much in common with both the Antiochene approach represented by such as Chrysostom, and with the Alexandrian approach of Origen and his admirer, Gregory of Nyssa. He had most in common with his predecessor Athanasius, whose work on the Psalms we explored earlier. Clearly for both exegetical traditions, for all their differences, reading one's life in terms of the biblical material was the most fundamental impulse, rather than particular interpretative

1. Karen Jo Tørjesen, ' "Body". "Soul", and "Spirit" in Origen's Theory of Exegesis', *Anglican Theological Review*, 67 (1985), pp. 17–30.

methods, and that way of reading had agreed practical implications. It meant upright moral living displaying the cardinal
virtues of the Greek tradition alongside the more characteristically Christian virtues of faith, hope and love. It meant an
ascetic lifestyle. And despite the distrust of 'passion', it meant
'falling in love with' the Word of God, becoming the Bride
of Christ. It is easy to see how the movement from typology
to allegory was so natural, and proved persistent despite the
reaction against it: the Antiochene Theodoret, like Origen
and Gregory, interpreted the Song of Songs 'allegorically' as
the love-songs of Christ for his church.

It is also easy to trace the movement from *mimēsis* to *anamnēsis* (memorial). The worshipper was caught up in a realistic
representation of the saving sacrifice of Christ which is most
inadequately regarded as mere imitation or mere symbol or
mere memorial. The eucharistic bread and wine, like the
blood of the Passover lamb, actually kept away the devil, the
angel of death, in both cases because they were 'types' of
Christ. On one occasion Chrysostom tried to elucidate the
paradox that there is one Christ who died once for all, and
yet countless and repeated celebrations of the eucharist: what
is offered, he affirms, is not a different sacrifice or even a
repetition of the original sacrifice, but the same sacrifice, an
anamnēsis of the same sacrifice, a 'replay', *mimēsis* or representation.

So Cyril's sacramental view of the scriptural text coheres
with patristic theology of the sacraments, and with his own
developing Christology: for Cyril was no docetist, and his
insistence on the One Nature of the Word Incarnate was
never intended to deny the reality of the flesh which made
the Word available to hungry souls. The life and liturgy of
the church was the contemporary embodiment of the Word
embodied in scripture. The present was meshed in with the
past by *mimēsis* and by empathy. This spirituality was both
individual and corporate, passionate and beyond passion.

Historical criticism treats eisegesis as anathema, and has
therefore been inimical both to allegory, and to the kind of
spirituality that seeks identification by imagination with those

148

who feature in the stories of Jesus. A retreat leader once commented that he found people could not use the Bible for contemplation if they were involved in biblical study for a Theology Degree. It is easy, if sad, to see why that has been the case. All forms of spirituality demand some kind of meshing of 'our story' with the biblical story, and reading ourselves into the texts inevitably involves procedures which have seemed unacceptable, a kind of *allēgoria* or description of one thing under the image of another.

As we have seen, it is characteristic of literary texts to draw the reader or audience into their world, partly by exploiting emotional identification, partly by presenting an image of the real world which clarifies understanding of that real world. This is not just Aristotelian theory, but the experience of novel readers who know that the world of the text is a fiction and yet profoundly true to human existence. Somehow the 'image' by abstracting from the total complexity of things, focuses the essentials, and by embodying 'types' in imagined particularities, evokes recognition of important 'universals' in human experience, usually involving relationships, moral claims, dilemmas within conflicting loyalties. In the very act of selection and rhetorical construction, the telling of a story whether fictional or factual, becomes such an 'image' of reality, and may so highlight claims upon us that our lives are involved and changed by the challenge. By a fictional tale, Nathan made David see the truth about his own action: "Thou art the man!" Things could never be the same again after that recognition.

Awareness of these dynamics immediately blurs the sharp distinction between historical and fictional narrative, for both are a *mimēsis*, and both have a purpose that goes far beyond mere cataloguing of events. Historical narrative is itself a 'construction' and for ancient historians it was meant to be a 'possession for ever' – like tragedy it had a moral purpose. Biblical narrative has the same persuasive intention: it is meant to draw people into the world of the text, give them a sense of their own identity, to challenge and change. The Bible is no more a textbook of the 'facts' of history than a textbook of the 'facts' of science. As literary texts, the books of the Bible are inherently 'figurative'.

Furthermore, language itself is plastic and its use and interpretation requires subtlety. "Our language is constantly telling us that something is what it is not."[1] The notion that one can confine oneself to the 'literal' meaning of the Bible depends on an exact correspondence theory of language – the letter of the text refers precisely to the world outside it as a matter of fact. As we have seen, the 'literal' meaning is more complicated than that, and in fact even scientific language uses metaphor and analogy, turning vocabulary drawn from ordinary life into technical terms (though sometimes this is obscured by the long-standing custom of using Greek or Latin roots instead of the vernacular!).[2] Language lies on a spectrum and does not fall into neat classifications. Much of our every-day language consists of 'dead' metaphors, and a teenager who insists on taking language 'literally' either drives his parents to distraction, or keeps the family constantly amused, depending on the spirit in which it is done! It would seem that to a very large extent language is by nature ambiguous, as the Stoics suggested. Metaphor and double meanings are the stuff of jokes and poetry.

So is personification. Ancient rhetoric discussed this 'figure of speech' self-consciously, but long before it had come naturally to Homer, and in a different cultural context, Proverbs 7–8 had described folly as a harlot, comparing and contrasting her with wisdom: each in their own way is depicted graphically as a seductive woman. When metaphor and personification are extended, a whole imaginary world may be constructed, a plot with characters interacting, but intended to have metaphorical force, referring to something other than what it appears to refer to. Once this kind of literary figure is under way, it will embrace varying degrees of artificiality depending upon the degree of comparability and incompara-

1. Jon Whitman, *Allegory: The Dynamics of an Ancient and Medieval Technique*, Oxford, 1987.
2. An excellent examination of metaphor as a linguistic phenomenon, and of the use of metaphor and model in science and religion is provided by Janet Martin Soskice, *Metaphor and Religious Language*, OUP, 1985.

bility. Fable and parable exploit this imaginative technique – it occurs in the popular story-telling of many cultures, and in the Bible itself when trees discuss the appointment of their king (Judg. 9:8–15). It is a short step from this to Ezekiel's riddle of great eagles and a vine growing from the seed of a cedar (Ezek. 17), to four great beasts being destroyed before a son of man appears with the clouds (Dan. 7), and seeds being scattered broadside and producing a range of bad and good crops (Mark 4:3ff and parallels). Clearly these visions and tales refer to something other than their surface reference. Allegory is born.

But there is allegory and allegory. There is compositional allegory, where the author's intention is to enlarge the techniques of projection or metaphor in this way, and where any other interpretation would not be true to the 'genre' of the text. There is interpretative allegory, where, irrespective of the intention, the text is read as representing a world other than the world explicit within it. As already noticed, all literary texts imply some expectation that the reader will correlate his or her world with the world of the text, so that its *mimēsis* implies and evokes some measure of *allēgoria*. But that perception does not demand the crass expedient of unpacking every item in the text as corresponding to something else. The attempt often leads to breakdown as incomparability increases and implausibility stares us in the face. The problem is that judgments will vary as to the validity of the original insight when this kind of breakdown occurs. But insights arising from imaginative engagement with the text are implied by the text's existence and survival. Some degree of allegory is inevitable. The problem with most allegory is that it is too much like an explained joke: if you have to explain it, it falls dead flat!

But interpretative allegory begins with insight, and then exploits techniques like etymology and explanation of assumed personifications self-consciously to bring texts into relationship with a perceived view of the world. Such techniques were already developed before the rise of Christianity, notably by philosophers like the Stoics. In their kind of reading, the Homeric gods become 'causes', and "all of mythic narrative constitutes for the Stoics a single, modulating voice, like the single, vibrating chord of the cosmic lyre".[1] So it was that language began to be regarded as having a "pervasive duality", as being naturally ambiguous, and the path was laid for connecting levels of allegorical interpretation with levels of being.

One of the charges brought against Origenist allegory is that it is arbitrary and has no working criteria. Many different meanings can be read 'out of' or 'into' a single text, and much seems to import a world utterly alien to the world of the biblical text. But this is to see only part of the picture. Origenist allegory was controlled by a view of scripture's unity and consistency which allowed the exploitation of texts from all over scripture to throw light on one another and build up a working-model of a spiritual world to which biblical images consistently referred.

Origen's pioneering work was taken further by later scholars such as Didymus the Blind, who exercised an enormous indirect influence on medieval exegesis through Jerome. Didymus appears to work with carefully established principles of interpretation. First there is a 'philological' examination of the logic and structure of the text in the external world, whether it has a factual or historical meaning. Then Didymus proceeds to ask whether the text should be understood as figurative discourse, consistently working with figures such as Jerusalem = Church to probe possible deeper meanings. Finally he discusses whether such figurative language signifies some other order of reality, whether it has reference to the spiritual world.[2] Such a hermeneutic lies behind the work of Cyril of Alexandria to which we referred earlier.

So the Origenist tradition of allegory relates to a Platonic view of two orders of reality, the 'lower' of which systematically represents by *mimēsis* the 'upper': the dual meaning of texts relates to those two worlds, 'sensible' and 'spiritual', distinguishable and yet united. It might seem that the situation is more complicated: for Origen spoke of three senses

1. Whitman, *op.cit.*
2. See J. H. Tigcheler, *Didyme l'Aveugle et l'exégèse allégorique, son commentaire sur Zacharie*, Nijmegen, 1977.

of scripture, medieval exegetes of four, neatly summed up in the mnemonic:

Littera gesta docet, quid credas allegoria
Moralis quid agas, quo tendas anagogia

The literal sense teaches what happened, allegory what you are to believe, the moral sense what you are to do, anagogy where you are going.[1]

However, the fundamental distinction is between letter and spirit, shadow and reality, the 'extra' meanings being a more sophisticated development of that underlying duality, as Origen's exegetical practice soon reveals. So the fundamental question about traditional allegory is whether such an understanding of the way things are remains sufficiently plausible to sustain such a method of interpretation. Can we presuppose the precise coordination of the 'sensible' world with the 'spiritual' world implied by Origenist allegory? Can we deduce the 'furniture' of heaven from its *mimēsis* on earth and distil spiritual truth from an assumed double meaning of the scriptural text?

Most people nowadays would instinctively answer in the negative. The existence of a supernatural dimension which is really more real than our everyday experience has seemed increasingly implausible to the modern mind, and the metaphysical basis for that kind of 'Two Natures' view of scripture has collapsed. We are also distinctly unattracted by an apparently 'static' view of things. But some of our examples of patristic allegory have shown how far from static conceptions they in fact were: as often as not, allegory was about 'journeying' into a dynamic relationship. And even if we eschew a Platonic dualism, perhaps some kind of allegory remains important because it alone gives spiritual depth and density to the text and to the world.

Indeed a kind of allegory which is less of a system and more of an intuition, a discernment of the fact of *mimēsis*, is

1. Quoted from Andrew Louth, *Discerning the Mystery*, Oxford, 1983, p. 116.

surely indispensable for the Bible to function within Christian spirituality. Every time a congregation sings "Guide me, O Thou Great Redeemer, Pilgrim through this barren land," an act of reading 'ourselves' into the biblical story takes place, and the desert is allegorically related to our experience – in fact we speak unblushingly of 'wilderness experiences' using a metaphor that is almost 'dead' it is so common. The impulse of allegory is such imaginative engagement with the text, an act of inspiration whereby the Bible 'rings true' to the world we live in, enabling us both to 'live in the world of the text', and to live in our own world in a new way.

Such 'inspirations' are bound to be various. Different genres within scripture will call forth different kinds of correlation, because of their different types of *mimēsis*. Different people from different cultures will find their experience 'chiming' with the Bible in different ways. No rules can be prescribed, and eisegesis is likely to be more than merely a temptation – rather a constant and inevitable reality. Judging what is legitimate will require much wisdom. The criteria for ruling out unacceptable interpretations will be difficult to establish. Coherence with the thrust of the overarching biblical story, or with the New Testament's criticisms of the Old, may at least provide a starting-point within the Christian community, disallowing piecemeal or unbalanced appeal to particular texts or the kind of exclusive appropriation of biblical privileges implied by such religio-political theories as apartheid. The long-standing images, symbols and metaphors of the tradition may also provide guidance. But the consensus of the community, while guiding the improvisation of the performer, might so confine it that new insights became unlikely, and prophetic or reforming criticism of the community's assumptions, even if inspired by the Bible, might become impossible. On the other hand, the performer might forget his or her fundamental rootage in the themes provided by the text and the tradition. A sensitive two-way process, on-going debate and dialogue about what is legitimate, is inevitable.

Yet for all the difficulties, some element of imaginative 'play' is surely necessary. For the texts are intended to 'persuade', and to rule out the possibility of eisegesis is to truncate their potential to persuade, to engage the mind and feelings of reader or hearer, to inspire action in the world. With an appropriate sense of *mimēsis*, the inspired exegete will enable human experience to be illuminated by a kind of divine destiny, and typological, Christological and doctrinal interpretation to be complemented by moral and spiritual response, both in the individual and in the community, issuing in the *praxis* of love: for according to Augustine, "scripture teaches nothing but charity . . ."

This chapter has attempted an exploration of what it means to 'live in the Bible'. It has touched on many interrelated themes, but has revolved around the issue of *allēgoria* in the widest sense of reading one thing in terms of another. This has impinged upon the corporate liturgical life of the Church as well as the individual spiritual journey, on the emotions and the transcending of the emotions, even on ethics and lifestyle. For in the tradition of spirituality stemming from the Bible, emerging as it did out of the struggle with Gnosticism, anything entirely 'otherworldly' had to be a false 'performance'. So the two worlds apparently implied in the Alexandrian allegorical tradition should never have been divorced. The spiritual 'meaning' is 'incarnate' in the text rather than belonging to an entirely different order of being, and so the performance of the text involves performance in the whole of life. So body, soul and mind, passions and intellect, together find peace and salvation in the Logos of God, and as Augustine noted, love proves to be the entire content of the divine communication: you cannot claim to love God and not love your neighbour.

Something similar can be said about music. It not only requires involvement, response, 'doing' not just 'reading', but it has even been said of music, as of the Bible, that love is its content: "Music is the imagination of love in sound. It is what man imagines of his life, and his life is love."[1] Furthermore, its transcendent or 'spiritual' nature is inseparable from its

1. W. J. Turner, quoted in Barzun, *cit.sup*.

physical expression, a point well highlighted by ancient theory.

The ancients thought that music, like other arts, was mimetic. But in what sense is music 'representational'? Music is rarely 'literally' mimetic: Beethoven insisted that his Pastoral Symphony was not a reproduction of outdoor sounds, including birdsong and a storm, but a recollection of the 'feeling' of being in the country, and Berlioz mocks the notion that music significantly imitates sounds like nightingales, rain or battles – it is only approximate and only significant if it is 'emotionally' appropriate. Musical depiction is to be distinguished from what Berlioz called musical metaphor:

> Of certain other compositions one may say that they represent a broad expanse or infinity itself, because the composer has been able to suggest to the ear, through the breadth of his melodies, the grandeur and clarity of the harmony and the majesty of the rhythm . . . impressions analogous to those a climber might feel on the summit of a mountain when beholding in space the splendid panorama suddenly enrolled before his eyes. And here too the truth of the image will appear only if the listener has taken the pains to inform himself ahead of time about the subject treated by the musician.[1]

In other words, music's ability to 'imitate' is poor, whether literally or metaphorically. What kind of thing was meant then by the music's *mimēsis*?

When the ancients spoke of music's *mimēsis*, they were anticipating the idea already noted that music represents the harmony of the spheres, the cosmic music heard by God alone. It is a persistent idea, found right up to the Nineteenth Century: "Music is the fragrance of the universe, and to capture it for his works the artist must, by loving and faithful study of the harmonies that float on earth and in heaven, identify himself with the mind of the universe."[2] Pythagorean

1. Quoted in Barzun, pp. 69ff.
2. Mazzini, quoted in Barzun, *op.cit.*

philosophy had linked the physical proportions of musical sounds with the regular movement of the planetary spheres, and suggested that number was the musical basis of the cosmic order. Whatever music was taken to 'represent', it was not a different world, but the world understood as incorporating, however imperfectly, the perfect ideals of mathematics. The parallel with other 'spiritual' realities was exact. Mathematics was the purest form of intellectual thought the ancients could imagine: it was natural to think that the music of the universe silently played in the mind of God.

As in early Christian doctrine, so in early Christian spirituality the mind of God, the Logos or Word, was both inherent in God and expressed in the cosmic order. The human mind was made in the 'image' of God's Logos, and knowledge of God was the supreme rationality, reached via an understanding of other spiritual realities such as mathematics and music. The so-called 'mysticism' of the Alexandrian and Cappadocian Fathers was profoundly intellectual: it began as a somewhat Platonic search to purify the self of the distractions of the flesh and the passions, so as to achieve that intuitive grasp of God which was open to the attuned mind through its kinship with the divine, but was enhanced by the perception that there never could be complete grasp of a Being in principle infinite.[1] As we saw at the beginning of this chapter, knowing God meant entering the darkness. This was a progress that sought to transcend the emotions, to reach *apatheia* or passionlessness, to fill the purified mind with the Logos of God. Like music, the Logos meant order and harmony.

But music is inescapably passionate, and paradoxically this 'knowledge of God' was also profoundly erotic, the loving response of a soul pursued by the outreach of the divine Logos in creation and revelation, incarnation and passion. The theological quest for understanding, increasingly defined in corporately accepted doctrine, was inseparable from the spiritual quest for union with God. The One who was in principle

1. See F. M. Young, 'The God of the Greeks and the Nature of Religious Language' in *Early Christian Literature and the Classical Intellectual Tradition*, in honorem R. M. Grant, ed. W. R. Schoedel and Robert L. Wilken, *Théologie Historique 53*, Editions Beauchesne, 1979.

impassible, submitted to passion for passionate love of his creatures, and sought to persuade to a passionately committed response of love. The complexity of this double movement is not well-served by the distinction between *agapē* and *erōs* traditional since Nygren.[1] Nor is it appropriately divorced from the corporate, liturgical life of the worshipping church, still less from the practice of ascetic and charitable living. As we suggested above, body, soul, mind and spirit were integrally involved in response to the loving persuasion of the Logos in search for his bride.

And that means that the caricature of patristic thought which suggests that they worked with a simplistic dualism of soul and body, or of the spiritual and the physical, has to be challenged.[2] In most instances, their theology was better integrated than that. Nemesius, writing on the *Nature of Man* reflects the complex awareness of the interaction of body, soul and mind in current philosophical and medical theory, while the Platonist Gregory of Nyssa married the idea of the resurrection of the body to the assumed immortality of the soul. In relation to the incarnation, they all struggled to express the doctrine that, like music, the Logos was incarnated in the physical, in real flesh like the real sound-waves made by real cat-gut or real leather stretched over real sounding-boxes. The 'Two Natures' coinhere.

The ancients recognised that like music or drama, the Logos moves the hearer to response, playing upon feelings of pity or fear, soothing out harried spirits, taming frenzied and disordered souls, and they knew that like music, the Logos brings rationality and order to the understanding. It is because the whole is meshed together as God's whole creation that two apparently distinct mimetic worlds never really worked, even for the Fathers. Music 'represented' the deep reality of the cosmic order, not a different world. Likewise whatever scripture 'represents', it is not a different world, but

1. *Agape and Eros*, ET Philip S. Watson, SPCK, 1932, 1938, 1939; republished 1982.
2. See F. M. Young, 'Adam and anthropos: a study of the interaction of science and the Bible in two anthropological treatises of the Fourth Century', *Vigiliae Christianae*, 37 (1983), pp. 110–40.

our world understood as God's. In that sense the 'Two Natures' coinhere, and the 'spiritual meaning' is inseparable from the letter.

Rather more than the Fathers, we live conceptually in one world, but dare we let it become merely one-dimensional? If music be wholly itself yet both physical and spiritual, why should not scripture too speak with a human voice yet 'allegorically'? Why should the Word of God not be incarnate in real human sentences on real fragile papyrus, vulnerable as Christ was vulnerable to whatever the human race might choose to do with it? Despite textual difficulties, put there to encourage the reader to search for the deeper meaning, "Origen declares the whole Scriptural record to be God's symphony, wherein the inexpert listener may think he perceives jarring notes whilst the man whose ear has been well trained realises the fitness and grace with which the varied notes are worked into one harmonious composition."[1] We are invited not just to hear but to respond, to listen to the voice of our Beloved, and filled with exultation sing our love-songs. For that is spirituality – thinking, feeling, and acting in love, and singing praises to our Divine Lover. When we sing love-songs we may use the classic scores of scripture or tradition, or we may make our own improvisations. But the themes are universal.

1. R. L. P. Milburn, quoted by Louth, *op.cit.*

8

Improvisation and Inspiration

Improvisation is essential to the proper performance of a cadenza. To quote *Everyman's Dictionary of Music*:[1]

> Originally the cadenza was simply a cadence: but the custom gradually established itself of creating a feeling of suspense between the chords of a cadence by interpolating brilliant passages of greater or less extent and at the same time giving the performer a chance to display technical gifts and inventiveness in improvisation.

The Dictionary adds that "Cadenzas are now rarely improvised, but supplied either by the composer himself or some other musician", but comment on the breach of principle simply proves its original importance. We will assume that our performer prefers not to 'regurgitate lecture notes', or present someone else's work as her own! She is singing her own love-song.

In order to improvise effectively, the performer not only has to have technical competence, but also needs to understand musical theory, the rules of harmony and counterpoint, the accepted conventions of development, the stylistic character of the work within which the cadenza is to figure. She has to have a sensitivity to the actual score of that work, its form, its themes and subjects, and their 'generative' potential. In other words she needs the equivalent of the philological competence of the biblical interpreter, linguistic skills, sensitivity

1. Ed. Eric Blom, rev. Sir Jack Westrup, Dent, 1953, 1977.

to context, and ability to re-state without distortion but with imagination.

A cadenza conventionally occurs within the performance of a classic concerto. The soloist performs in the context of a community of players. The 'quotations' in the improvisation need to 'mimic' the way they were played by members of the orchestra to ring true to the total performance. So there is a two-way process of 'listening' and 'speaking'. In the cadenza the orchestral players are silent, but ideally not uninvolved: the whole community is caught up in the performance, helping to evoke the best from the soloist, as the score of the classic (or the text of the tradition) is developed for this unique occasion.

So the climax of the concerto is the cadenza. The orchestra pauses, the soloist takes off in a sparkling display of improvisation. But it is no good if it is simply a firework show of technical brilliance. It must be integrated with the 'given' score, though a development of it, and it must engage others in the unity of the whole. On the one hand, the soloist is able to produce a show of skill, and without the performer's total involvement – indeed projection of her personality – the cadenza would be dull and uncommunicative. On the other hand, the soloist is the servant of the music – bringing out what is potentially there in the themes and harmonies of the original score. If that is not the case, the cadenza will not 'belong' to the performance of this particular classic.

But the performance is not just for the members of the orchestra: it is for a particular audience in a particular hall at a particular time. Peculiarities of acoustics, or audience reaction, may affect the performance very deeply, including the rendering of the cadenza. The performer is a kind of bridge between the 'classic' work and the audience, and a rigid bridge will crack under pressure.

As in the case of any other allegory, strains are likely to appear if it is pressed too far. But what we have described applies also to the performance of the Bible. The orchestra is the community of the faithful, and with the soloist its members perfect the performance in rehearsal. Ultimately the audience is the world. Just playing the old classic without a cadenza is like reading the lessons without a sermon. It is true that reading well depends on good translation and interpretation, but only the preaching enables proper development of the classic themes for a new situation. It is no good simply replaying the old cadenzas, because each generation has to appropriate the themes anew, and the renewal alone can effect communication. In order to improvise these essential new cadenzas, which will inevitably be somewhat ephemeral, the preacher needs skills, philological skills, hermeneutical theories, imaginative insights, and a lot of sensitivity to context. The bridge has to be flexible or it will crack under pressure.

The skills are acquired by attending music-school and doing the necessary practice, in other words, reading textbooks and listening to the great masters of the art, and submitting to tutorials as if they were Master-classes. Ideally modern scholars and theologians in the lecture-theatres are the facilitators of performance, and they are honoured no more by adulation or slavish discipleship, than by rejection and scorn. They seek to inspire a critical *mimēsis*, a desire to create appropriate improvisations and play skilful new cadenzas in new situations. For the bridge to be secure, each performer needs to create her own cadenza for the situation in which she finds herself. The performer, not just the composer, needs inspiration, and the old tradition that the Holy Spirit is necessary for proper interpretation needs to be reclaimed. It is not just a matter of acquiring technical skill, nor is it just a matter of skills in communication and in projecting personality. The inspired 'musicality' of the performer has to be fostered by bringing the old score and present experience into creative interaction.

Pluralism is a feature of modern music as of modern Christianity. It is difficult not to be drawn into making judgments about content, style and significance, and not at all easy to acknowledge the value of those 'genres' or 'performances' which are not to our taste. But some measure of catholicity in musical taste is emerging among young people, and the ecumenical movement would seem to encourage a similar development in Christian circles. The problem, however, is that the issue concerning proper 'performance' of the Bible creates such suspicions that it splits groups apart within and across the historic divisions of the Church. Those sold on the 'historico-critical' approach to exegesis can be just as dogmatic about what is permissible as those who insist upon 'verbal inspiration'. But if plurality of performance is a fact of life, may it not be both appropriate and creative? True, any and every performance may not be fitting, but that does not mean that there is only one possible approach. Respect for other people's performances may be the starting-point of renewed inspiration.

But the present pluralism means that discordant voices will immediately be heard when the idea of a cadenza is mooted. We can imagine the following dialogue:

A. We cannot possibly entertain the idea that a cadenza is necessary. As far as we are concerned, all we need to do is to replay the classic texts: for the Bible contains the truth, the whole truth and nothing but the truth. As with a recording, we only have to put on the disk and press the button, then identically the same authoritative rendering as always will be heard.

B. But you overlook the fact that a genuinely 'neutral' performance has never been available. Only 'live' performances were feasible till this century, and every 'live' performance is different, as any great artist will tell you. Nowadays new technologies have improved the instruments used in modern performance, and communication in ever new environments has affected what is communicated whether we like it or not. To see the earth spherical on satellite pictures relayed to a television screen and hear voices from speakers in a room on one's own, is to be presented with physical and social horizons that pose profound questions about how to perform the old biblical repertoire. The ideal of a single authoritative rendering is unrealisable: we may be able to use a recording these days, but there is no 'neutral' performance, however traditional.

C. But just as we can make some attempt to 'realise' an old music score, so we can simply 'read' an ancient text, and however mechanically, simply or traditionally the task is done, something is heard. It happens like this in churches everywhere, and it is a kind of performance, though without a cadenza. It surely cannot be summarily dismissed as useless. The main problem is that only those already committed to it will give it the attention it deserves, and communication is unlikely to occur except when people have 'learned the language'. But with all these new translations about, and all these marvellous charismatic songs which just put lively tunes to favourite biblical texts, a cadenza is not so necessary after all.

B. That position is quite unacceptable: in fact, if it comes to that, never mind about playing a cadenza which relates in style and theme to the classic concerto – that is far too old-fashioned and culture-bound! What we suggest is this: entirely new music is needed. In fact modernity and historical criticism have destroyed the possibility of performance, save as a matter of antiquarian interest.

C. What you overlook is the problem of loss of identity, the danger of syncretism. You deserve to be faced with the conservative reaction. Christian communities need the classic texts of Holy Scripture because their 'normativity' is largely what makes those communities Christian. The canon is one of the few things all groups claiming to be Christian have in common. They meet to play their classical chamber music. You radicals may form new ensembles, or choose to go it alone, but you cannot expect to remain part of the community if you abandon the community's roots. Of course we cannot prevent your experiments getting some hearing, and no doubt you voice some justifiable dissatisfactions. But your way is ultimately destructive.

D. Of course, we older people in the churches, and some younger ones too who share our conservative cast of mind, really like a 'classic' performance with a 'classic' and familiar cadenza. We find anything new and unusual too disturbing.

C. So performance of the Bible has for its cadenza 'hymns'

inherited from the Reformation, or Wesley, or the Oxford Movement, which are replayed in denominations or 'party'-churches over and over again. True each such cadenza was originally an imaginative development of the biblical themes, and is still worth playing, but repetition has become more important than renewal, and the attempt to plan an ecumenical concert ends up having to include recognisable features of these old cadenzas, often in abbreviated form for lack of time and imagination. In their own right they may remain worth preserving in full, and can be given fresh performance, but surely we need new cadenzas too.

E. What we really want is the classics turned into 'Pop': Bach with modern rhythms goes down well, so why not steal the best tunes from the devil and put biblical words to them? The basic truths are comfortably unchangeable, but they can do with being made more fashionable, and then they can get a hearing in the commercial world of the mass media. As in the world of music, so in the world of religion the pops can get finance behind them, and that can only be to our advantage.

C. But on the whole pops are short-lived and superficial. True a pop song occasionally catches depth through simplicity, or speaks out of the heart of an indigenous culture, and such moments are to be valued. But often such material settles at the level of cliché, leaving the listener undisturbed. A recent newspaper article drew attention to the comfortable predictability of rock music, compared with the more demanding creativity of a classic like Mozart.

E. But addiction to Mozart can induce the same unthinking stupor through sheer familiarity. And sometimes that is the kind of 'peace' we need. Religion, like music, is properly used in therapy, both with individuals and groups. And pop is very effective for this. You can dispense with elaborate cadenzas, and just jazz up the classic themes.

F. What I like is stuff from other cultures – so exotic and interesting. We Westerners are blind to things in the Bible that Africans understand, like genealogies and sacrifice and the way stories give communal identity. And the base communities in Latin America prove that very ordinary people anywhere can read the Bible and see how to live within its world, without all this specialism and élitist education. Surely we can learn so much by listening to their ways of performance.

C. The trouble with your kind of fascination is that it is patronising and short-lived. Most Westerners can be fascinated by Indian Ragas for five minutes, but then find it difficult to concentrate. It is simply too hard to recognise there what we find familiar. Certainly we may learn something from other cultures, and certainly the vitality of biblical interpretation among ordinary people has an important contribution to make. But we cannot escape our own struggles to work out what cadenza to play in our own situation – including the post-Enlightenment intellectual world.

D. But we need to beware of novelty. Novelty in music simply fails to communicate. Take electronic music – most of us have no way of grasping what it is about because it has no long-standing public tradition, and we have no corporate memory, no 'categories' with which to follow it. And if it comes to that, much contemporary music which strives to be classical is too novel and lacks an audience. Like much modern theology it passeth the understanding of the uninitiated. It communicates with nobody.

C. I wonder why. Is it because we are mostly lazy listeners, and prefer the familiar? A 'contemporary classic' is a bit of a contradiction in terms, but what modern music and modern theology seek to provide is something like that – a cadenza which both has a recognisable relationship with the style and themes of the classics of the past, and has found a way of speaking in modern idiom so as to persuade an audience whose minds have been affected by modernity. The dilemma is how to play a modern cadenza in biblical style, or a biblical cadenza in modern idiom. Almost inevitably one or the other end of the bridge gets out of balance.

Such an imaginary dialogue makes the point clear: we have

to take risks, and we have to expect different artists to have a go in different ways. There is bound to be improvisation if we are to sing love-songs that are at once our own, and yet inspired by, and integrally related in theme and style to the classics provided by the repertoire we have inherited. How is this demanding task to be done? And how is the result to be 'persuasive'? In what sense are the classics 'normative' or 'authoritative'? How are we to live with the fact of pluralism?

Different types of cadenza have been played in Twentieth-Century theology. Clearly there is not enough space here to embark on a lengthy discussion, but a brief review of the analysis provided by David Kelsey in his book, *The Uses of Scripture in Recent Theology*[1] may forward our discussion. That Christian theology is done 'in accordance with scripture' is the presupposition which makes widely divergent theological proposals relevant to this enquiry. Kelsey demonstrates that the senses in which scripture is taken to be normative or authoritative for theology vary considerably, but in some sense scripture is summoned up to 'authorise' theological proposals, and the way this happens depends on how a particular theologian 'construes' scripture. This confirms, by analysis of modern theology, the point we made earlier about the necessity of 'frameworks' within which scripture is interpreted.

Kelsey uses seven 'case-studies', selected precisely because they reflect different ways of construing scripture. He asks of each such questions as what aspect of scripture is taken to be authoritative and why, and how is scripture brought to bear on theological proposals so as to authorise them?

His first case-study selects an example of a theologian whose position we recognise as 'fundamentalist'. The Bible is treated as a numinous object, entirely and in every detail inspired by God. This is supported from the Church's experience and from the content of scripture itself, the classic texts being 2 Timothy 3:16, 2 Peter 1:19–21 and John 10:34. Kelsey points out that the procedure implies that the authoritative

1. SCM, 1975.

aspect of scripture is the doctrines it teaches, and that salvation depends on believing those doctrines. The reason for these doctrines being authoritative is that scripture is inspired, and this is a 'hypothesis' that cannot depend on empirical verification. It arises from the fact that scripture is holy in the experience of the church and itself teaches this doctrine.

Such an approach to scripture depends on construing scripture as absolutely distinctive, as belonging to one kind of 'genre', and then 'abstracting' its doctrinal content by deduction from the text. Basically the same procedure is found in his second case, a typical representative of the 'Biblical Theology' school. The Bible contains distinctive 'concepts' enshrined in characteristically biblical terms. Word studies purport to show how these concepts differ from Greek ideas for which the same words are used. A process of deduction similar to the process of deducing doctrine makes the supposed 'content' of the Bible distinctive and authoritative, and turns biblical language into a system of technical terms. As Kelsey says, the similarities in these respective theological methods are striking, and indeed important given their apparently opposed starting-points, the one accepting historical criticism, the other not. Both take scripture as authoritative because of some intrinsic property of the text.

Kelsey suggests that in cases like these dependence on scripture is 'direct', but in important ways they are at one remove. Because scripture is construed in a certain way, and therefore the texts are set within a particular interpretative framework, and because the content of scripture is encapsulated in doctrines or concepts deduced from the text, both of these approaches are 'cadenzas', whether they like it or not. They are similar in procedure to the patristic cadenzas which deduced such doctrines as the Trinity from the 'data' found in the Bible. The aim of this procedure is to communicate what is thought to be the content of scripture, to persuade the hearer to respond to the content so as to believe or to live in a certain way, and both types which follow this procedure have in practice had a measure of success in building the communicative bridge. But the particularities of the text are inevitably submerged or forced into conformity with the 'framework'. It is impossible to take up narrative or poetry into discursive 'doctrine' or 'concepts' without loss.

Kelsey's next case-studies highlight another way of construing the authority of scripture. Scripture functions as the medium whereby the 'presence' of God, or Christ, is made real. That is what it means to speak of scripture as revelation. It is not that scripture reveals doctrines, but it reveals a 'Person'. He begins with G. E. Wright and the book which was once so influential, *The God who Acts*:[1] "God is . . . known by what he has done." "The Bible is not primarily the Word of God, but the record of the Acts of God, together with the human response thereto." It is "recital, in which Biblical man confesses his faith by reciting the formative events of his history as the redemptive handiwork of God". 'Propositions' and 'ideas', in other words doctrines and concepts, cannot deal adequately with the biblical material.

Wright, like A. S. Peake, was a biblical scholar, indeed an archaeologist, and he felt compelled to construe the Bible in the light of empirical evidence. So the particularities of the text, at least as record of events, were given proper due, but 'authority' was located in the agent behind the events behind the text rather than the text itself. Wright's 'theory' is not unlike the older view of 'progressive revelation': God reveals himself in action and relationship, and has to limit himself to developing human capacity.

So the idea of a distinctive 'salvation-history' was developed as a way of appropriating the biblical material, which was understood to be the 'kerygmatic' recital of the past into which people are called and which gives present believers their identity. This history reveals the character of the God who calls, so "theology is the discipline by which the church, carefully and with full knowledge of the risk, translates Biblical faith into the non-Biblical language of another age". So the revelation is to be understood in dynamic rather than substantialist terms. Yet here again a process of deduction is involved: what is deduced is the 'character' of the God who

1. SCM, 1952.

169

appears in the narrative record, and ironically, as Kelsey points out, that character is summed up in 'concepts'.

But narratives can provide 'identity descriptions' by 'rendering an agent', and this is the way scripture is widely used by Karl Barth. The story makes the character 'come alive', and so the humanity of Jesus has to be understood in terms of a 'history' rather than a 'nature'. His acts are *his* acts, enactments of his intentions, and so they constitute his identity. In the same way, the divinity of Christ is explicated in terms of anecdotes that show what he is like: the resurrection is his 'self-declaration'. So what gives the Bible its unity is the fact that it renders the same agent, God. This is a much more subtle and convincing way of seeing the Bible as revealing the character of a Person rather than doctrines about him. The Bible functions as revelation when someone encounters God through its 'performance'.

For Barth the true 'subject' of theology and of scripture is the incarnate Lord, and only in so far as scripture and theology communicate that Person through narratives about him is it persuasive or 'authoritative'. Kelsey suggests that this is a 'hypothesis' as untestable as the 'hypothesis' of plenal inspiration, and yet it would appear to be a good description of how the Bible largely functions in the Church. For most Christians, the 'king-pin' of scripture is Christ, and all the rest is judged against the picture they have of his teaching and his character. That picture is by no means simply a 'historical reconstruction' on the basis of careful sifting of evidence – rather it is a complex amalgam of impressions created by performances influenced by tradition and interpretation.

Such use of scripture is clearly the creation of 'cadenzas', but cadenzas not unrelated to the themes and traditional patterns of performance we have reviewed in the patristic material. At the same time, such cadenzas have their particular style and emphasis affected by modern concerns, concerns with history, concerns with the nature of personhood. Even more explicitly 'modern' is the approach of Bultmann: the existential encounter with Christ is the essence of the matter, and there is no need to worry about the difficulties presented

170

by the 'primitive' dress in which the biblical faith is presented. Such ideas can be 'de-mythologised' and 'translated' into modern idiom. The Bible is authoritative in so far as it facilitates this saving encounter, and promotes 'authentic existence'.

Alongside Bultmann, Kelsey places Tillich and L. S. Thornton, demonstrating how each sees scripture as authoritative in so far as it expresses a revelatory and saving event of the past and occasions its occurrence for someone in the present. They differ sharply in their analysis of what 'modern man' needs to experience salvation: Bultmann's emphasis on human subjectivity is diametrically opposed to Thornton's 'cosmic' perspective. But their understanding of what the Bible is supposed to 'do', Kelsey finds fundamentally similar. The Bible is construed as an 'expression' of saving event, which can be reproduced, "whether its expressive force is said to take the form of literary image, religious symbol or kerygmatic myth".

Clearly if Kelsey were doing his analysis now, there would be other candidates for inclusion – people like Pannenberg, Moltmann, the Liberation theologians, to note just a few. One suspects, however, that the process of analysis would turn up similar conclusions. What determines the role of scripture in a theologian's work is the way in which scripture is construed as a whole, and this is deeply affected by the experience and concerns which are brought to the text.

For much modern theology the issue of history has presented itself as either a challenge or a key. Historical consciousness has sharpened the sense of history's particularities – the fact that the past is different from the present, and people's understanding of themselves, their relationships and their societies is culturally diverse over space and time. Post-Enlightenment suspicions about the 'historicity' of much biblical material containing miracle and myth have also deeply affected biblical scholarship and theological reflection. Pannenberg is an example of a theologian for whom Christian theology is primarily to do with history. But he is not alone. For many modern scholars and theologians the Bible is about God's relationship with history. It is important to realise that this is a modern 'framework', only loosely paralleled by patristic concern with God's relationship with the created order: it was the denigration of the 'material' which encouraged docetism and Gnostic otherworldliness which made the Fathers insist on the real 'history' of God's dealings with humanity culminating in Jesus, and this is a far cry from the kind of questions and concerns that our modern sense of history poses.

Moltmann would seem to have 're-discovered' eschatology for modern theology, and in a sense he has. What biblical scholars found by paying attention to the texts had been regarded as problematic, incompatible with a modern outlook, part of the ancient 'mythology' to be re-expressed. But Moltmann is not simply playing biblical themes. His cadenza is effective because it construes scripture in the light of modern experience and modern political drives to create a better world. His collection of sermons, *The Power of the Powerless*,[1] is a series of 'cadenzas', sometimes more, sometimes less directly related to the biblical text, always aware of the implications for modern believers and so presenting a two-way process. Liberation Theology is quite explicit: we begin with the present situation, with the need for *praxis*, and we read the Bible in the light of that.

This confirms one of Kelsey's conclusions: that it is a mistake to think that what modern theologians, and indeed modern interpreters, are doing, can be described as 'translation'. The process is much more complicated than that, and our image of 'improvisation' is much closer to giving an account of how the Bible and Modern Theology relate to one another. It is perhaps not quite so 'indirect' as Kelsey would have us believe, because undoubtedly biblical themes, harmonies, features, images, styles – even specifically quoted texts – contribute to the cadenza, but new combinations arise from reading the text imaginatively in the light of actual experience.

Hermeneutical theory as interpreted by Werner Jeanrond[2]

1. ET SCM, 1983.
2. *Text and Interpretation as Categories of Theological Thinking*, ET Gill and Macmillan, 1988.

spells out more technically a similar conclusion: reading is more than deciphering signs on paper – it is a dynamic process in principle open-ended, in which the reader has an effect on the text, and the text an effect on the reader. The way the text is read must be appropriate to the text and its genre, and every reading is a response to a textual claim, yet there is no such thing as a neutral, innocent, a-historical reading. Reading is conditioned by the cultural, social, religious, political, 'image' context of the reader, by the reader's reading norms acquired through education, by specific reading interests, as well as by the text being read. In a sense a text does not exist until it is read – like a musical score, it only has potential until it is 'realised'. So that its 'reading genre' may be different from its composition genre: reading in a particular context puts it into a functional framework, so Paul's letters acquire in a liturgical context a different function from when they were direct epistolary compositions 'posted' to his churches. Cadenzas are inevitable, and so is a plurality of readings.

The real problem with many past proposals has been their 'exclusivity', their assumption that they know what 'modern man' needs, their assurance that they have a full account of what 'encounter' with God is like, their presupposition that they have provided a convincing 'translation' by 'deducing' the truth about God from the revelatory material. Theologians look for an 'organising principle', and overlook the fact that defining the authority of scripture means confining it. What they have got right is the need to engage with the assumptions of 'modernity' and the problem of playing the biblical themes when the 'classical' harmonic structure has broken down. As Kelsey points out, it takes an act of imagination – or to put it in our terms, it involves inspired creativity, or improvisation.

So how does the Bible function in practice? Kelsey provides a useful account: "Part of what it means to call a text 'Christian scripture' is that it functions to shape persons' identities so decisively as to transform them", and it does so "when it is used in the context of the common life of Christian community":

Scripture is authority for theological proposals not by being the perfect source of the content that they fully preserve, but by providing a pattern by which the proposal's adequacy as elaboration can be assessed. The elaboration of the pattern involves both reasoning and imaginative insight to see just how it may be elaborated to meet new situations and problems faced by the Christian community.

Elaboration, or improvisation, is unavoidable, and the diversity of genres, patterns, paradigms which scripture embraces is of fundamental importance, for it allows many different cadenzas to be played.

The Bible itself, in other words, speaks in many different ways, and its variety of genres means it can have a multiplicity of functions. It is a record of events in which certain witnesses were caught up, a collection of prophetic oracles, and a form of address persuading the reader to certain courses of action, sometimes through proverbs, sometimes laws, sometimes parables. It is a revelation of truth, the truth about human failure and corruption as well as the truth about God, and also the presentation of a way of life, of a challenge and a call. It is a collection of prayers and hymns, and of human attempts at making sense of things, the human search for wisdom. It is all these things and more.

If the Bible speaks in different ways, it will be 'authoritative' in different ways: theories are usually too narrow to account for what happens in practice. There are real problems with pressing the whole Bible into one controlling genre such as law, prophecy, doctrine or even the fashionable one, narrative. The variety of patterns of biblical expression provides a "limited range of determinate possibilities for construing the mode of God's presence", and the whole collection a "set of different but quite determinate patterns, any one of which might be elaborated in new theological proposals". The canon as a whole provides controls by determining ways in which these various paradigms relate to one another. Jeanrond similarly sees 'classic' texts as providing 'paradigmatic perspectives' and the canon as 'one pluralistic norm'.

"Theological proposals are concerned with what God is

now using scripture to do – and no degree of sophistication in theological methodology can hope to anticipate that," affirms Kelsey. So "theological criticism is guided by a *discrimen*, not a 'norm' or a 'criterion' ". By *discrimen* Kelsey means "a configuration of criteria that are in some way organically related to one another as reciprocal coefficients". In other words, the exercise of judgment, sensitivity and imagination is indispensable; or as Jeanrond puts it, classics are not exempt from critical assessment. So biblical criticism must have a role to play. Kelsey suggests that exegesis may be approached in different ways: it may be a matter of purely historical or literary interest, or it may be a self-conscious treatment of the texts as scripture. Only the latter has any intention of explicating a 'normative' meaning. Yet the other approaches set limits and plays a role in arguments about theological proposals. Biblical scholarship is relevant though not in any way decisive. There is no hope of a perfect hermeneutical key or control: pluralism is inevitable.

So there are bound to be many cadenzas, and judgments have to be made as to their respective adequacy. Biblical texts "play a necessary role in passing judgment on the Christian aptness of current churchly forms of life and thought and on theological proposals about how to reform them". As Jeanrond puts it, the text 'provokes' response. But there is an inevitable process of dialogue and debate between readers, and a necessary enrichment from hearing many different performances. A schoolgirl performs Strauss' Horn Concerto brilliantly. Comparison with a recording by a master performer will no doubt reveal a certain immaturity, but that does not detract from the brilliance of her particular performance on that particular occasion. Nor does her performance detract from the illumination provided by the master-performance. Too often performances of the Bible which do not suit us are dismissed as too naïve or too élitist. We need the humility to listen to one another's cadenzas with respect as well as criticism, for there is richness in diversity – as recent biblical scholarship has been reminding us.

One thing we have suggested throughout this study is that a

particular construal of scripture needs to work with parameters parallel with those of Christology. Account has to be taken of 'Two Natures' which coinhere. We may usefully review the adequacy of different 'cadenzas' against this criterion.

The kind of approach to scripture which deduces doctrines or concepts from the text (Kelsey's first two types) faces a danger somewhat similar to the Eutychian heresy – the 'humanity' is liable to be swallowed up in the divinity. Because of assumptions about the inspiration of scripture and the use of 'proof-texts', the 'indirectness' of the approach has been generally overlooked, and of course such procedures were anticipated by those whereby the early church arrived at the 'classic' doctrines of Christianity. Yet the danger remains. Those who have no taste for this kind of performance have easily been able to point to the difficulties involved,[1] but the underlying 'ineptness' in relation to the shape of Christian doctrine has usually gone unremarked.

The problem lies in the fact that the particularities and diversities of the text are either taken up into an aura of holiness that demands mere subservience, or they are allowed to drop away into insignificance compared with the distinctive compelling concepts or doctrines that are to be directly appropriated. This kind of method rejects the genuinely new possibilities created for construing scripture by our modern historical consciousness, and reverts to the persistent 'docetism' which Christianity has constantly had to challenge within its ranks. The 'nitty-gritty' of the complex range of material in the repertoire is ignored, and a genuine 'incarnation' made impossible because the 'flesh' is not taken seriously enough.

This is connected with an inadequate theory of inspiration. In the ancient world there were a number of different conceptions of 'inspiration'. The Pythian priestess at Delphi was 'taken over' by the god Apollo, who spoke through her, she being simply an instrument of the god's communication. As

1. e.g. James Barr, *The Semantics of Biblical Language*, OUP, 1961; *The Bible in the Modern World*, SCM, 1973; *Fundamentalism*, SCM, 1977.

noted in an earlier chapter, the orthodox reaction to Montanism was to accuse it of sharing such pagan notions of inspiration, and one extant saying uses the pagan analogy of a lyre being played by the Spirit. In scripture, this kind of inspiration is attributed to 'ecstatic' prophets like those who infected Saul, and to the prophets of Baal, but is not otherwise found.

Doctrines which suggest that the Spirit 'dictated' the scriptures belong to a similar class. The Sibyls, unlike the Pythia, composed verse oracles in their own person, but under the guidance of the inspiring god or daemon; their oracles were written down, prized, collected and consulted throughout antiquity, and eventually preserved in 'Christianised' form.[1] 'Dictation theories' can find some scriptural precedent in the instructions given to Ezekiel and John to write down the message they received, but when used to suggest that every little detail of scripture carries the same numinous quality, they have a Sibylline ring, and they have their origin in the fact that in Hellenistic times the Jewish scriptures were treated as collections of oracles like the Sibylline books, as evidenced in the Qumran material and early Christianity.

The assumption that 'doctrine' or 'church structure' or 'ethics' can be directly read off the page of scripture is what has made Protestantism inherently fissiparous, and it is evident that this approach lacks 'Christian aptness'. The "humanity is subsumed in the divinity". Such a doctrine is not true to the 'classic shape' of Christian teaching, and it tends to isolate the scriptures from their place in the whole spectrum of Christian understanding: is it holy books, or the Church which collected them, or Christ, or any one of these without reference to the others, that has the 'primary' authority? Yet there is an appropriate place for a certain exaggeration of the tradition that scripture is the Word of God in the face of the opposite tendency – so to exaggerate the historical difficulties and human fallibilities evident in the text as to

1. H. W. Parke, *Sibyls and Sibylline Prophecy in Classical Antiquity*, Routledge, 1988.

appear to exclude any inspiration at all. The Jesus of John's Gospel is not recognised as coming from God by his opponents: he is a man making absurd and blasphemous claims. Sometimes the opponents of fundamentalism look a bit like those who are treated in the Fourth Gospel as blinded. Yet that Gospel itself bears witness to the difficulties of keeping a genuine hold on the reality of the 'flesh' when the glory is painted too brightly. There has to be a genuine tension, a real possibility of treating the scriptures as 'mere literature' until the 'signs' are interpreted aright.

It might seem that the way scripture is construed by Kelsey's third case fits that requirement more satisfactorily. What is revealed in scripture is the character of God, for scripture is the record of his acts, written by particular people as testimony to their response of faith. Do we not have here an acknowledgement of 'Two Natures' in scripture in a way analogous to Alexandrian or 'kenotic' Christologies? Do we not also have a more 'Christianly apt' understanding of inspiration – namely one in which the 'prophet' retains his personality, speaks in his own person, and freely communicates what God has revealed? Surely 'progressive revelation' or 'salvation-history' meets our requirements.

Again people who do not like this kind of performance have been able to find cogent arguments against it: philosophically the notion of God's direct action is peculiarly problematic, especially in the modern world which is so deeply affected by scientific understanding of the way things work and hostile to any resort to a *deus ex machina* – in Bultmann's terms such thinking is 'mythological', and the Fathers would have treated it as far too anthropomorphic.

But the fundamental problem with this as a way of construing scripture is the fact that scripture is subordinated to events outside itself, and becomes the expression of human response rather than God's Word in itself. The priority of the 'community' or the 'people of God' who responded to his revelation and produced the scriptures, continues to be a very common way of coping with the difficulties posed for 'Holy Scripture' by modern historical method, and it is not in essence very different from these earlier proposals which for one reason or another have been found to be wanting.[1] In the end, so far from being analogous to a 'kenotic' Christology, they turn out to be like a kind of 'adoptionism', or at least to have the faults the Alexandrians detected in Nestorian Christology – the 'divinity' is only indirectly involved because the humanity is the subject of all the 'incarnate' experiences.

The Bultmannian approach is even more evidently Nestorian. As has often been observed, Bultmann revels in divorcing the Christ of faith from the Jesus of history – what matters for faith is not the particularities of history but Christ's universal relevance for authentic human existence. To grapple with the actual particularities as a historian and with the meaning as an existentialist produces a clear 'dividing of the natures'. Bultmann is not alone: Kelsey rightly links others with him. For the problem with much modern theology is that it 'begins' from anthropology, and works 'from below', so scripture 'begins' as a human book, and understanding it as the Word of God in any immediate sense becomes difficult. The reasons for this are clear, namely the features of 'modernity' with which modern theology has to be engaged, its sense of human 'historicity' and 'autonomy'.

By contrast the neo-orthodox movement stimulated by Karl Barth confronted 'modernity' with the self-revelation of God through his Word. Again opponents of this kind of theology have found good reasons to criticise it, not least because of its somewhat cavalier attitude to the findings of historical criticism, and its apparent 'throw-back' to a pre-critical world. However, Barth's dialectical theology is only comprehensible as a radical critique of 'modernity'.[2] Ultimately Barth recognises that all theology, like all religion, is a human construct, and to it he opposes the 'otherness' of God. "Revelation means in the Bible the self-unveiling to us of the God who essentially cannot be unveiled to us," and yet God's will to be one with us in Christ expresses his very nature. Christology is the pivot around which Barth's thinking revolves in such a way that the particular historical 'being'

1. e.g. John Barton, *People of the Book?* SPCK, 1988.
2. As shown by Jenson in *The Modern Theologians*, ed. David F. Ford, Blackwell, 1989.

which God freely chooses to embrace, is understood to be constitutive of his very nature as Trinity. Here we find a genuinely incarnational or Alexandrian Christology which then sees scripture as bearing witness to that key event in such a way as to be itself the medium of revelation, the Word of God. So the presence of God is 'incarnate' in the process of communication.

But modern 'Antiochenes' may justifiably suspect that such an incarnational theology compromises the 'human-ness of humanity' in particular, but also the 'Godness of God' – it runs the risk of an Apollinarian 'mixture' of the natures. Such a performance is impressive, but we need other performances to bring out the distinction of the 'Natures', to do justice to the 'fleshliness' of the text alongside the reality of God's 'accommodation' to our level. Surely the Bible is revelatory not just of God in Christ, but of the sinfulness of humanity: we have to read ourselves into the text so as to be convicted – Barth himself would surely agree.

Another model of inspiration might be artistic inspiration. Artistic inspiration was regarded in the ancient world with the same kind of aura as prophetic inspiration – it had the marks of the divine, and 'good' art, whether poetry, drama, music or sculpture, was almost exclusively religious. Like prophecy, art has an inherently 'ambiguous' quality: everything is a 'symbol' and 'meaning' is indeterminate because different possibilities are inherent in the creative medium. The artist's experience is of 'inspiration' being beyond personal conscious control and sometimes in spite of herself. Yet the artist produces her own work. The response of hearer or reader is more than merely passive since the 'recipient' of the 'revelation' has to discern in the 'symbol', the meaning or meanings that ring bells or create new discernment. The authority of such artistic creation is inherent in the work, and yet has no impact on the 'blind' or 'deaf' – only on those who see the signs and believe.

Like all analogies, such a model has its problems: 'Can it do justice to the "uniqueness" of scripture?' will be the question asked by those who ask the parallel question about the uniqueness of Jesus Christ: indeed this was exactly the problem the Alexandrians had with Antiochene Christology – it seemed to reduce the incarnation to something akin to the inspiration of a mere prophet or sage. Others will wonder whether our analogy really accounts for the fact that we have no clear 'author' for much of the biblical material – rather the texts are community products, the result of long processes of formation. Others will justifiably deflect the charge of pagan sources in this direction. But pagan or not, it hints at the potential 'universality' of the Bible, and it has the advantage of doing justice to the 'humanity' of the text as well as its 'divinity', and to the fact that these two 'elements' are inseparable from one another. It gives an account of why every performance is inadequate: for all fall short of the potential of a great work of art. It allows for the fact that all readers do not in practice respond in the same way, and the 'hearing' is selective: in a concerto some elements form a backcloth, but the discerning ear may pick out significant lines of music from individual sections of the orchestra.

So Bultmann's performance is 'one-dimensional', like hearing just the oboes speak. And the major options in modern approaches to the Bible and theology are each abstractions from the whole complexity of the text and of human existence: is it subjective experience, or the dialectic of social forces, or both of those and many other things, that shape our lives? Even the preoccupation with historical particularities, with distinguishing fact and interpretation, proves to be a dualism that fails to do justice both to experience and the text: for it tends to exclude the aesthetic, the imaginative, the 'spiritual' as necessarily 'mythological' and fantastic. A proper appreciation of artistic 'symbolism' could help us to regain an appreciation of the coinherence of two realities in one universe.

There never can be a definitive performance if the scriptures present us with a Christ who is both the fulfilment of all the complexities of our existence and a critical challenge to it. Nor will there ever be a single adequate 'doctrine' of biblical authority or a single adequate 'theology' of biblical inspiration. Like 'faith and works', 'grace and freewill', and many other areas of Christian thought, the truth does not lie where the tension or paradox is resolved. Only as the struggle to 'perform' Christological and sacramental theology adequately bears upon the struggle to 'perform' Holy Scripture will we begin to appreciate the range of dynamics we need to exploit. The 'parameters' within which discussion and exploration take place are provided by the 'Chalcedonian' structure of Christian understanding, but critical discussion of a plurality of attempts will always be required. Through dialectic we move on, but the theological task is in principle infinite and beyond human capacity. Scripture itself provides paradigms of pilgrimage, of progress and set-back, of faith and hope, rather than concepts, doctrines or definitions.

Furthermore, the texts themselves point forwards, referring not just to events of the past, or to present experience, but to the future, often a visionary future guaranteed by partial anticipation in present experience, known by faith not sight. And that future, we are promised, is one of 'performance', of playing harps, of worship. The Lamb of God slain before the foundation of the world lies on the altar in heaven awaiting our participation, and sacramentally is given to us on earth as a foretaste of the heavenly banquet through bread and wine which is itself yet more than itself. Like music, the Word of God is never just 'back there', tied to an antiquated score in an unread library, experienced as alien, as discerned across a great gulf or hermeneutical gap: it is 'realised' in performance, a performance inevitably inadequate at present, yet an earnest of the great eschatological performance to come in God's good time.

A MOZART CONCERTO

Playing their heart out
flute and harp
harp and flute
the tools of heaven's
chief occupation.
Our preoccupation
to sing and play
play and sing

music being itself
a taste of heaven.

The kingdom of heaven
for Barth
Mozart
who only sings and plays.
No message
no heartsearch
simply the praise
the joy
of created things
just being themselves.

But where's the fiddle
no place for a fiddle
no place for me?
And where's the oboe
no place for an oboe
no place for those
who can't manage
the flute
or the harp?

Never fear.
The kingdom of heaven's
for all
for all
who just sing and play
playing their heart out
orchestrally
communally
in harmony
the sound of heaven's
chief occupation.
Spirit-inspired preoccupation
to follow the maestro
singing and playing
playing and singing
beyond expectation.

We didn't know
we had it in us
to play and sing
to sing and play
so radiantly
so accurately
so precisely together
in harmony
each performing
our own vocation
each rapt up
in a symphony
beyond ourselves
in the kingdom of heaven
playing our heart out.

Back on earth, I lie relaxed, and whether waking or sleeping I know not, I find myself back in the second violins of a student orchestra. And I know I cannot cope. My technique is not up to it. The manuscript on the music stand is in places illegible. The difficulties in performance are so great I want to run away and hide.

But I keep the bow moving in the same direction as everyone else, and hope to escape notice. I know my playing will never be any good. The music begins to sound familiar, however, and its themes and harmonies begin to take hold so that the problems cease to fill the forefront of my mind and the embarrassment of self-concern begins to drop away as listening and concentrating takes over. The work begins to come alive, to seem entirely fresh while deeply familiar. Just being there gets exciting. The gaps and illegibilities seem to ask to be filled in in appropriate ways because the 'flow' of the music carries us along. True I cannot play every note, but still all of us begin to lose ourselves in the rhythm of the movement, subtly responding to the plastic beat of the conductor's arms. The soloist joins us, and the conductor's face reflects the glow of his bright warm tone. We dance along caught up in this festive performance, till our bows draw out that hanging, expectant chord, and we wait poised for the cadenza:

> A memory of Kreisler once:
> At some recital in this same city,
> The seats all taken, I found myself pushed
> On to the stage with a few others,
> So near that I could see the toil
> Of his face muscles, a pulse like a moth
> Fluttering under the fine skin,
> And the indelible veins of his smooth brow.
>
> I could see, too, the twitching of the fingers,
> Caught temporarily in art's neurosis,
> As we sat there or warmly applauded
> This player who so beautifully suffered
> For each of us upon his instrument.
> So it must have been on Calvary
> In the fiercer light of the thorns' halo:
> The men standing by and that one figure,
> The hands bleeding, the mind bruised but calm,
> Making such music as lives still.
> And no one daring to interrupt
> Because it was himself he played
> And closer than all of them the God listened.
>   R. S. Thomas[1]

Perhaps it is supremely at passion-tide that our preoccupations with principles and problems are superseded by a sense of what *mimēsis* and *anamnēsis* really mean. The story cannot escape the particularities of history, but as Gadamer puts it:[2] "Aristotle is right: poetry makes more visible than that faithful narration of facts and actual events which we call history can ever do." It enables "a form of participation that is beyond the reach of contingent reality with all its limitations and conditions". So *mimēsis* does not mean a

---

1. 'The Musician' from *Tares* © R. S. Thomas 1961, reproduced by kind permission.
2. *The Relevance of the Beautiful and other Essays*, CUP, 1986, p. 129.

realistic or literal imitation: rather it is an 'ordering' which allows self-recognition. It is a 'sign-language', with an inherent ambiguity which allows for symbolic representation. "Music, perhaps the most sublime of all the arts, has taught us for centuries that such a thing is possible. Every composition of 'absolute music' possesses the structure of undecipherable (or indeterminate) meaning."

So it is not simply the particularities of history that matter, but the capacity of the story to become a sacramental *anamnēsis*, and the characters in it to become 'larger than life' so as to illuminate our lives, so that the whole takes on a universal quality and reveals the glory of God in the midst of the tragedy. And the illumination produces captivation, and captivation means contemplation, and contemplation brings discernment, and discernment means involvement . . .

So the cadenza comes to an end, and the orchestra plays its heart out, rehearsing the glory of God which "will flame out, like shining from shook foil", from that series of badly written dots on a crudely ruled page.

Epilogue

A Good Friday Performance for Radio

Where shall we begin?

With the empty boredom of a ritual repeated every year?

Or with expectation at the possibility of a fresh performance, a living drama that makes visible the invisible?

The problems of celebrating Good Friday are not unlike the problems of theatre, problems explored by the great director Peter Brook in his book *The Empty Space*. For an act of theatre, all that is required is an empty space and a spectator. The crucial question is what happens in that empty space and what is communicated to the spectator. Theatre may be, indeed often is, deadly. What makes it deadly? Peter Brook's answer is complex, but it includes the constant unchanging repetition of a classic, and the lack of expectation in the audience. If a drama is to live, it must be constantly renewed, constantly re-presented, and always assisted by the expectant involvement of the audience.

The passion-story is one of the greatest dramas. But tradition has fossilised it, and piety removed it from confrontation with life. Believers are so anxious to preserve its fixed status as an event of history that its true potential as living drama, ever-changing, ever-new, is undermined. We dare not tamper with the text. We dare not go beyond the literal meaning. And so we miss more than half of the truth.

Suppose we now create an empty space, and let the drama be re-enacted: maybe we will discover that we cannot bear too much reality.

> An empty space becomes the stage of life
> Filled with the play of weeping without end.

Drama cannot happen except through strife.
So women weeping for sons and lovers tend
Their graves. Weeping for innocent victims slain –
The first-born in Egypt, Bethlem's toddler sons –
Resounds in the Gulag. Torture's twisting pain
Exhilarates. There's fun in games with guns.
There is no consolation for Rachel's grief.
There is no Messianic peace, but a sword.
Women weeping, weeping without relief.
Daughters of Zion, do not weep for the Lord.
Weep for yourselves and your children. "Father, you
Forgive them; for they know not what they do."

Tragic drama arose as a religious ritual in classical Athens.
The great philosopher Aristotle tried to analyse the effect
tragedy has. He came to the conclusion that it effected
katharsis – purification. We tend to think this means a great
"emotional steam-bath", as Peter Brook puts it. But for Aristotle, *katharsis* was a religious word. How then is *katharsis*
achieved in religion? As the anthropologist Mary Douglas
explains in her book *Purity and Danger*, primitive peoples took
things that were taboo, things like blood and death, and
by putting these fearful things into a sacred ritual context,
transformed them from being life-denying to life-affirming.
That is what sacrifice is all about. That too is how tragedy
works: it makes it possible for human beings to avoid escap-
ism, to confront those things they dare not face. Normally we
cannot stand too much reality, but here we can.

What's it about – this strange drama dispensed
In emptiness – this strange king not a king,
Judge not a judge, offender without offence?
Why does this passionate suffering action bring
Catharsis, despite its ambiguity?
Weeping and fear, involvement and dread,
The deep darkness of shared identity,
A chill tingling creeping over the head
And cold tremors shivering down the spine
Bring strange purgation. It's holy mystery

That intimation of sin line by line,
Disclosure of corporate corruptibility,
A powerful catalyst of hope should be –
"Today in Paradise you'll be with me."

And so there is 'Holy Theatre': "We are all aware," says
Peter Brook, "that most of life escapes our senses." "We know
that the world of appearance is a crust – under the crust is
the boiling matter we see if we peer into a volcano." In
theatre "the invisible becomes visible", and it is possible to
find liberation from our normal everyday selves. This is what
makes "the theatre a holy place in which a greater reality is
found". Often it is found in the paradox of a loss which is
also gain.

The woman weeps, weeps at the foot of the cross.
What a waste of a life – what promise bites the dust!
What purpose, meaning or sense is there in this loss?
Is it enough to reflect what must be must?
"Woman, behold your son. Your mother, son,"
He rasps, and harsh the voice of reality:
It's no good clinging to me, woman, I'm done.
Mother instead my beloved community
That's in the world not of the world, but new.
Woman, my hour has come. Don't cling to me.
Her human anguish he cannot thus subdue.
Love possessively clings to empathy.
Loves proves itself by seeming most distressed,
And yet – the pain of joy pierces her breast.

Great tragedy probes for the meaning behind it all. The
tragedies of the ancient world found meaning in a sense of
destiny. Mark's Gospel, though its language is the crude
rough Greek of a Palestinian, is written with unconscious
literary art. The central figure of the drama is progressively
isolated, misunderstood, betrayed by a friend, denied by his
right-hand man, despised, mocked, rejected, finally forsaken
even by the God whose will he strove to perform. Yet Mark
makes clear that this is the playing out of a destiny long

foreshadowed – in ancient prophecies, in terrible tales like the sacrifice of Isaac. The Son of Man must suffer. The Son of Man goes as it is written of him.

> The weeping of a father for his son
> Lain on the altar as a sacrifice.
> The agonising cry, "Thy will be done" –
> No explanation ever could suffice:
> Why, O my God, O why? Face to face
> With the dark horror of humanity
> A cry of desperation puts his case,
> "Why O God hast thou forsaken me?"
> The drama's climax is his isolation
> Deserted by the crowds, betrayed, denied,
> Friendless, alone, he faces desolation.
> In ultimate abandonment he died.
> So where was God? A strangely present absence,
> Weeping, emptying out his very essence.

For John's Gospel, the passion is a fulfilment, a triumph staged by the hero himself in which everyone else unconsciously fulfils their destiny. It's as though the pattern of an ancient ritual is played out for real: the king submits to humiliation, defeat and death on behalf of his people, then to rise up, vindicated by God, assured of victory for the future. The crowds celebrate the festival. There is a glorious triumph. As Matthew puts it, the veil of the Temple is rent in twain, tombs open and the dead rise. The hour of glory has come. The task is accomplished. The Son of Man is lifted up and draws all men to himself.

> "I thirst," he cries, for vinegar and gall.
> He has to take the way of destiny,
> To enter that abyss on behalf of all,
> Patterning the struggle on prophecy.
> The king of the Jews plays out the testing role
> Of victim exposed to the people's enemies,
> Exposed to judgment, cut to the very soul.
> The people play out unconscious destinies –

They part his garments casting lots. They wag
Their heads at him, deriding him, and rave,
Come down from the cross. His limbs begin to sag.
He saved others, himself he cannot save.
He trusts in God, let him deliver him.
The answering darkness is a silence grim.

"It's finished." The joy of fulfilment fills full up
To the point of choking. The curtain's rent in twain.
The universe rises, applauds, lifting the cup
Of celebration on high, its cheeks tears stain.
I if I be lifted up will draw
Everyone to myself in my moment of glory.
After each curtain call a call for more –
No-one dare let go this spacious story,
This passionate actor acting out a passion,
Performing by submission, controlling events
By loss of control, and apparently perdition.
The stench of death makes incense-breathing scents,
Suicide sacrifice and death new life.
Atonement cannot happen except through strife.

And so the drama effects an exposure of the truth – the truth
about humanity. Out of the crooked timber of humanity, said
the philosopher Kant, can nothing straight ever be made. Yet
by exposing that truth and facing it in a ritual context, the
thing that is taboo can be turned into something holy, the sin
we cannot bear to face can be redeemed, and atonement
effected. This is the work of God. Only in the empty space
created by God can a resolution of human strife be played
out. Only in the empty space that *is* God can the drama be
truly holy and the invisible made visible.

The play demands the spaciousness of God,
an emptying of God that's no retreat
From bearing stigmata, scars slashed by the rod
Which empties human pride of self-conceit;
The weeping of a king riding an ass
Yearning like a hen to mother her chicks;

191

The hooligan act of human hate en masse
Stringing him up exposed on two crossed sticks.
Inevitable the way of destiny:
Ironical judgment judges the judge of all
And judged itself is made a mockery.
The violence and innocence appal.
God's empty space alone transcends our limit.
"Father into thy hands I commit my Spirit."

"There is no doubt that a theatre can be a very special place," says Peter Brook. "It is like a magnifying glass, and also like a reducing lens. It is a small world, so it can easily become a pretty one. It is different from everyday life so it can easily be divorced from life." Christians have always 'put roses on the cross' and made it pretty. Churches domesticate the story. Repetition robs it of its power. And the insidious power of piety blunts its cutting edge.

But a new production can raise expectations.

An expectant audience can create a new atmosphere.

And then the repetition becomes powerful re-presentation.

Priest and people will weep, weep for shame and weep for joy.

They will find cleansing in their tears.

For like the finale of Bach's *St Matthew Passion*, the tears are triumphant . . .

Index

Index

Kant 191
katharsis 139, 143, 188
Kazantzakis, Theodore 28
Keller, W. 103
Kelly, J. N. D. 48n
Kelsey, David 167–75, 178–9
Kermode, Frank 31n
kerygma 58, 60, 169
Kingdom of God 82–4
Kings, Books of 18, 28, 35, 76
Kinneavy, James L. 131
Koestler, Arthur 2–3
Koran 62, 107

Lampe and Woolcombe 74n, 77n
Langerbeck, H. 135n
language, biblical 123–6
, metaphorical 127–8
of scripture 90–1, 150
, religious 127
, symbolic 127
Lanier, Sidney 88–9, 104, 110, 114
Lash, Nicholas 21n
law 27, 29–30
, Jewish 29, 48, 101
Law and the Prophets, the 34–5
Leavis, F. R. 31n
liberation-theology 1, 104, 171, 172
linguistic theory 6–14
literalism and Bible 89–95, 104, 123, 128,
    150, 153, 187
literary-criticism 102, 137
literature, scriptures as 178
, study of 96–8
Lofthouse, W. F. 4–5
Logos 47, 86–7, 116, 119, 121, 124, 155,
    157, 158, *see also* Word
Logos-theology 57, 116, 118–19
Louth, Andrew 153, 159
love 155
lover, divine 136, 159
, image of 145
Luke, Gospel of 15, 35, 37, 41
Lutheran scholarship 16, 61

Mark, Gospel of 41, 81, 151, 189–90
Marcellinus 141
Marcianus 58
Marcion 36–40, 46–7, 54, 90, 102, 115
Mary 55, 78
Matthew, Gospel of 75, 101, 190
McKinnon, J. 3n
Melchisedek 75
Melito of Sardis 69–74, 78, 143
Messiah 70, 82, 90, 188

Messianic hopes 75
prediction 9, 76
reading 16
metaphor 90, 93, 97–8, 99, 150, 151, 154
methodikē 96, 98
Micaiah-Ben-Imla 75–6
midrash 18, 28
Milburn, R. L. P. 159
mimēsis 101, 108, 110, 137, 138, 140, 141,
    144, 146–9, 151–5, 162, 185
Modalists 116, 119
Moltmann 171, 172
Monarchians 118
Monogenes 47
monotheism 4, 30, 122
Montanus, –ist, –ism 40, 177
Morgan, Robert 7
Moses 27, 60, 67, 72, 92, 94, 119, 134
Mozart 113, 131, 165, 182–4
Muses and literature 42, 76
music in tragedy 139, 143
musical metaphor 2–3, 4–5, 22–5, 26,
    31–2, 36, 45–6, 66–7, 81–2, 86–7,
    88–9, 96, 104, 108–10, 111–15, 122,
    123, 129–30, 131–3, 136, 141–3,
    155–9, 160–7, 175, 181, 182–6, 192
Muslims 122
myth 7, 28, 47, 171, 178

Nag Hammadi Library 54–5
Nemesius, *Nature of Man* 158
Noah 60
Nussbaum, Martha 138–9, 140–1
Nygren 158

Only-Begotten, *see* Monogenes
Oracle, Delphic 75, 176
oracles 27, 47, 75–8, 109, 174
Oracles, Sibylline 75, 177
oral tradition 108
Origen 49, 84–7, 90–5, 98–9, 101–2, 104,
    106, 136, 147–8, 152, 159

Pannenberg 171
parable 99, 141, 151, 174
Paraclete 40, 41
Paradise 55, 60, 94
Parke, H. W. 75n, 177n
pascha 69, 73, *see also* passion *and* Passover
Paschal Homilies 78
passion 50, 69, 72–3, 185, 187
Passover 69, 74, 109, 143–4, 146, 148
patriarchal narratives 141, 146
patristics, *see* Fathers, early Church

196